The *Mystery* of the Church

UNVEILING *the* CHURCH *as the* BODY OF CHRIST

A STUDY OF EPHESIANS

Dr. Sim A. Wilson

The Mystery of the Church:
Unveiling the Church as the Body of Christ
A Study of Ephesians

ISBN: 979-8-9859232-2-3 paperback

Editing, formatting, and cover design services by ChristianEditingandDesign.com.

Contents

Preface

Never before has more been expected of the church than today. She has sailed into turbulent waters under most difficult and trying circumstances. The church today is being discredited. There is widespread distrust, disrespect, and disregard. The blundering human factor has at times brought the church to disrepute. Her spiritual authority and divine mission, once taken for granted, are now being challenged and even denied. She faces dangers from without and from within. It is time for believers to speak out boldly for the church. I want to declare myself at the very beginning of this study with three statements.

I believe in the Church!

The church organism and the church organization. The church spiritual and the church literal. The visible church and the invisible church. This is the church age, and all that God is doing, He is doing through His church. The church's mission and message are divine.

I am committed to the Church!

My church membership in the organism and the organized Body of Christ is a spiritual covenant which I guard with integrity. After more than seventy years of membership in the church, I still hold my commitment to salvation and Christ; to the Word and discipleship; to discipline and accountability; to faithfulness and loyalty; to leadership and submission.

I love the Church!

I love the church because of Who its founder is, the Lord Jesus Christ. I love the church because of what it is founded upon, the faith of Jesus

Christ. I love the church because of its absolutely certain future, for even the gates of hell cannot prevail against it.

The Apostle Paul speaks out boldly in the Epistle to the Ephesians regarding the nature and mission of the church as the Body of Christ. May hearts burn and hopes rise upon launching this in-depth study of this great epistle, making fresh discoveries about the church which is His body.

THE EPISTLE TO THE EPHESIANS
OVERVIEW

SUBJECT: THE MYSTERY OF THE CHURCH

KEY VERSES: "And gave him to be the head over all things in the church, which is the body, the fulness of him that filleth all in all" (1:21–23).

I.   INTRODUCTION:

Ephesians presents the mystery of the church as the body of Christ. It is a mystery because although a part of God's plan from the beginning, it was withheld from man's knowledge until God's special time to reveal it. The key word is "unity," with the thought of gathering together the fragmented human family into one body, the church, through Jesus Christ. Each chapter in Ephesians seems to point to a particular phase of the church.

II.   THE MYSTERY OF THE BODY (Chapters 1–3):

Chapter 1: Origination of the church in eternity past, revealing God's redeeming love for man; contains a doxology of praise for God's eternal plan and continues with a prayer for the believer's enlightenment.

Chapter 2: Formation of the church where the pit of human depravity becomes the scene of divine activity, and living stones are raised by divine workmanship into a spiritual masterpiece.

Chapter 3: Edification of the church in this passage shows God's church growing and developing from two primary sources: by the ministry of the Word and by the practice and power of prayer.

III.   THE LIFE OF THE BODY (Chapters 4–6):

Chapter 4: Vocation of the church is compared to a walk of faith pursued in unity of Spirit and to a walk of purity where we "walk worthy of the vocation wherewith [we] are called" (4:1).

Chapter 5: Separation of the church is demonstrated in an analogy of the Christian walk in which we become followers of God, walking in love, light, wisdom, and harmony in all the experiences of life.

Chapter 6: Preservation of the church is linked to the principle of mutual submission, and finally ends in total victory on the battlefield of faith using weapons of our warfare: the Sword of the Spirit and the weapon of prayer.

THE EPISTLE TO THE EPHESIANS
INTRODUCTION

KEY VERSES: "And gave him to be the head over all things to the church, which is his body, the fulness of him that filleth all in all" (1:22–23).

THE TEXT: "Christ is the head [first, authority] of the church: and he is the saviour [provider, protector] of the body" (5:23b).

THE SUBJECT: The Mystery of the church. It presents the mystery of the church as the body of Christ. "Mystery" in the New Testament sense is not something that cannot be understood; mysterious, and unknowable. It is a particular part of God's eternal plan known to Him from the beginning, withheld from the knowledge of men until God's special time to reveal it. Ephesians 3:2–3, 5 explains it as "the dispensation of the grace of God which is given me to you-ward: How that by revelation he made known unto me the mystery . . . Which in other ages was not made known unto the sons of men, as it is now revealed unto his holy apostles and prophets by the Spirit."

CENTRAL TRUTH: The key word is "unity," which conveys the thought of gathering together the fragmented human family into one body, the church, through Jesus Christ. The human race is fragmented, alienated, and polarized; separated from God, each other, and himself. Ephesians pictures God pulling mankind together, unifying them into one body, the church, through Jesus Christ.

INTRO: Ephesians claims a significant place among the epistles because it reveals the purpose of the church in the plan of God.

IT IS A SPECIAL LETTER.

Ephesians has been called the "Queen of the Epistles" because of its splendor in style and language. It is considered "Paul's third heaven epistle" because here is a glimpse of glory before the foundation of the world. It is thought of as "the Alps of the New Testament"[1] because it calls us to the holy mount of God's "spiritual blessings in heavenly places" (1:3). It is claimed to be "the Holy of Holies of Paul's epistles" because it takes us step by step into the manifest presence of God, revealing His plan and purpose in the church.

IT IS A PRISON LETTER.

Interestingly enough, it is one of Paul's prison epistles written while behind locked doors under severe persecution, probably about 60–62 AD. From here, he shares the revelation he has received of the mystery of the church. In prison he sees into eternity past when "before the foundation of the world" the church is planned by God the Father (1:4).

IT IS A CIRCULAR LETTER.

Every reference to "the ecclesia" applies to the church universal, and never to a local body of believers. And it does not address any existing problematic situation in the local body of believers. For these reasons, many scholars believe this is a circular letter meant to be shared in all the churches. It proclaims the eternal purpose of God, which is that in Jesus Christ divided humanity would be united and gathered together into one body, the church.

CONCL: The salutation: The first two verses contain an appropriate opening to the study of the mystery of the church. They introduce us to the highest office in the world: the saints and the faithful. The greatest paradox in the world: double residency in Christ and in Ephesus. The choice blessings in the world: grace and peace.

---

1   James A. Stewart, *The Alps of the New Testament: Ephesians* (Skyland, NC: Revival Literature, 2005).

The divisions: Ephesians naturally falls into two main divisions—the doctrinal section, which explains the mystery of the body, chs. 1–3; and the practical section explaining the life of the body, chs. 4–6. The epistle may be tied together with six strong words which, when applied to each chapter, will describe the establishment and development of the church: origination, formation, edification, vocation, separation, and preservation. We will study the epistle with one of these words for each chapter.

❦ Chapter 1 ❦

ORIGINATION: GOD'S ETERNAL PLAN OF SALVATION

Ephesians 1:1–23

INTRO: God's eternal plan is introduced with an enumeration of the greatest things in the world.

The highest office in the world, "an apostle of Jesus Christ" (v.1a).
The best people in the world, "the saints" and "the faithful" (v. 1b).
The greatest paradox in the world, "at Ephesus" and "in Christ" (v. 1c).
The choice blessings in the world, "grace" and "peace" (v. 2).

The truths of this chapter take the form of praise and prayer for our instruction.

I. THE GREATEST THINGS IN THE WORLD (1:1–2)

   A. The Highest Office in the World (v. 1a)
   B. The Best People in the World (v. 1b)
   C. The Greatest Paradox in the World (v. 1c)
   D. The Choice Blessings in the World (v. 2)

II. PRAISE FOR GOD'S PLAN (1:3)

   A. Praise is Natural to a Christian (v. 3a)
   B. Praise is Reasonable to a Christian (v. 3b)

III. GOD'S PURPOSE FOR YOU (1:4–6)

    A. God Has Chosen Us to be Saved in Christ (v. 4)
    B. God Has Predestined Us to Sonship by Adoption (v. 5)
    C. God Has Made Us Accepted in the Beloved (v. 6)

IV. CHRIST'S PROVISION FOR YOU (1:7–12)

    A. Christ Has Redeemed Us Through His Blood (v. 7)
    B. Christ has Revealed in Us the Mystery of His Will (vv. 8–10)
    C. Christ Has Rewarded Us with His Inheritance (vv. 11–12)

V. THE HOLY SPIRIT'S POWER IN YOU (1:13–14)

    A. The Sealing of the Spirit (v. 13)
    B. The Earnest of the Spirit (v. 14)

VI. THE PRAISE OF HIS GLORY (1:6, 12, 14)

    A. The Glory of God
    B. The Glory of Grace (vv. 6, 12, 14)

VII. PRAYER FOR GOD'S PEOPLE (1:15–23)

VIII. THAT GOD MAY GIVE—SPIRITUAL PERCEPTION (1:15–17)

    A. The People of God (vv. 15–17a)
    B. The Knowledge of God (v. 17b)

IX. THAT YOU MAY KNOW—SPIRITUAL ENLIGHTENMENT (1:18–23)

    A. What is the Hope of His Calling? (v. 18a)
    B. What are the Riches of His Inheritance? (v. 18b)
    C. What is the Greatness of His Power? (vv. 19–23)

I. THE GREATEST THINGS IN THE WORLD

*"Paul, an apostle of Jesus Christ by the will of God, to
the saints which are at Ephesus, and to the faithful in
Christ Jesus: Grace be to you, and peace, from God our
Father, and from the Lord Jesus Christ." (1:1–2)*

Ephesians 1:1–2

INTRO: Ephesians is "the Queen of the Epistles." It surpasses all others in splendor of style and language. "The Holy of Holies" of Paul's epistles. Here we enter the presence of God's Shekina Glory. Entranced by the beauty of the "rainbow round the throne." Enthralled by the brilliance of eternal light streaming through the opened heavens. Enthroned by Divine Grace to sit together with Christ in Heavenly Places.

Interestingly enough, it is one of Paul's prison epistles. It presents the Mystery of the Church as the Body of Christ. The church is a mystery because, although a part of God's plan from the beginning, it was withheld from man's knowledge until God's special time to reveal it. Every reference to the "Ecclesia" applies to the universal church and never to a local body of believers.

The key word is "unity". The key thought is the gathering together of the fragmented human family into one body, the church, through Jesus Christ. The world is fragmented, alienated, and polarized. Man is separated from God, each other, and himself. Ephesians pictures God pulling mankind together, unifying him in one body, the church through Christ. Divine reconciliation: at one with God, others, and self.

ILL: Paul had witnessed an *illustration* of this in the Roman Empire. Through the Roman Empire a new unity had come to the then-known world. The "Pax Romana," the Roman peace, was a very real thing in Paul's world. Kingdoms, states, and countries which had struggled and warred with each other were gathered into a new unity by the "Pax Romana."

Disunity in humanity. A unity in the Body of Christ. It is appropriate that this great book begins with an enumeration of the greatest things in the world.

A. The Highest Office in the World (v. 1a)

Here is the servant's double authority:

1. Christ's Messenger, "an apostle of Jesus Christ"; "apostle" Gr: APÓSTOLOS "sent one, dispatch, not his own but sent."

   a) It does not signify a class or office, but a calling, a ministry. Ministers ought to think more of fulfilling a call than of succeeding in a profession.
   b) ILL: When the Sanhedrin made a "dictum," or ruling, they sent out an APÓSTOLOS to spread the word.
   c) He is a messenger of the greatest person, "Jesus Christ." Messenger of the gospel. Employed by Jesus Christ. A sent one. All believers are messengers of Christ and the gospel.

2. Divine Authority, "by the will of God." This was a divine call, not a human choice. It was not by the will of men conferring an office upon him. Not by his own intrusion. He was a messenger by the will of God.

   a) He was commissioned by the greatest authority, "the will of God." There is no higher place in the world than "the will of God."
   b) There is no promotion to greater from "the will of God." Paul was convinced God had a plan for his life. Are you? He was "a chosen vessel unto the Lord."

B. The Best People in the World (v. 1b)

Here is the believer's double designation: "The Saints"; "The Faithful."

1. "Saints" Designates Our Position! "To the saints which are at Ephesus," "saints" Gr: HÁGIOS "holy one, righteous people, one recognized for his holiness." From God's perspective.

a) This is the world's grandest title. Called "saints" for their sanctity and righteousness.

b) It is an imputed righteousness. Imputed at Calvary. Imparted at conversion.

c) Saints are not a special class of persons exalted to sainthood by the church. All Christians are saints. Saints by the grace of God, not by some special order like canonization.

d) Some translate this word "God's people" instead of "saints." It is always plural, and never singular.

e) ILL: A little girl was asked, "What is a saint?" Remembering the stained-glass windows of her church, she answered, "A saint is a person the light shines through."

2. "Faithful" Designates Our Practice! "To the faithful in Christ Jesus." This is the saint's most glorious quality. God, make us saints. It is our part to be faithful.

a) There are no saints who are not faithful. Practice denies our position.

b) "Faithful" is a comprehensive word which always carries the meaning of "believers who are trustworthy."

c) The Faithful are those who trust Christ and are true to Him.

C. The Greatest Paradox in the World (v. 1c)

Here is the Christian's double residency:

1. In the Community Where He Resides. It shows a double residency: physical and spiritual. The Christian principle: "in the world but not of the world." In the world physically but not of the world spiritually.

a) Every Christian has double residency. He has a human address and a divine address. That is the secret to the happy Christian life.

b) ILL: I read of a lady who lived in constant hardships, yet she remained calm and serene. When asked her secret, "My secret is to sail the seas, and always keep my heart in port."

c) Wherever a Christian is, he is still in Christ.

2. In Christ Where He Dwells. The phrase occurs 130 times in the NT: "in Christ" is the source of the believer's life; "like Christ" is the goal of Christian maturity; "with Christ" is the fullness of our joy and hope.

   a) "In Christ" expresses the mutual relation of the believer to Christ. It does not mean faith in or believing in. We are "IN" Christ—living there.

   b) ILL: Like the root is in the soil. As the branch is in the vine. As the fish is in the sea. As the bird is in the air. So the believer is in Christ.

   c) ILL: This paradox is illustrated perfectly in the experience of an old country boy who was gloriously saved. He had the glow and shine of a brand-new Christian. God had given him a double dose of old-time religion. His folks thought he was crazy and sent him to a psychiatrist. Doctor asked, "Where were you born?" Answer: "I've been born twice; which time are you talking about?" Question: "What's your father's name?" Answer: "I've got an earthly father and a Heavenly Father; which one are you talking about?" Question: "Where do you live?" Answer: "I've got two homes, earthly and heavenly; which one are you talking about?" They say the psychiatrist became so confused, he had to go to a psychiatrist.

D. The Choice Blessings in the World (v. 2)

We are doubly blessed. What a way to greet anyone. Just add to our warm hellos and cold goodbyes, "grace and peace." The Roman-Greek world's parting wish was "safety." The Jews used a better one, "Shalom" or peace. The NT Christian greeting was "grace and peace." It is distinctly Christian. In the pastoral epistles it is "grace—mercy—and peace."

1. "Grace be to you!"

   a) Grace is the matchless gift of divine favor. It denotes three things: God's good-will towards us; His good work within us; and His great power upon us.

b) The use of the word "grace" Gr: CHARIS carries two main ideas:

    1) It describes the loveliness and attractiveness of the Christian life. Charisma. Appeal. Attractive.

    2) It means a gift which is impossible for man to secure for himself; he could never earn it and in no way deserves it.

c) Grace is everything: saved by grace; kept by grace; stand in grace; taught by grace; live in grace. It reminds us of where we came from and where we are in Christ.

2. "Peace be to you!"

a) Peace is the unsurpassed quality of spiritual serenity. Peace" Gr: EIRENE, Hb: SHALOM "union, union after separation, bringing together, reconciliation after a fight or quarrel." Grace is always first. Peace comes afterward.

b) There is no peace without grace. The Father is "the God of all grace" (1 Pet. 5:10). The Son is "the Lord of peace" (2 Thess. 3:16). Grace is the beginning of faith; peace is the end of faith. Grace is the fountain, springs; peace is the stream. Grace is the source, and peace is the result.

c) There is a peace with God. (See Rom. 5:1.)

d) There is a peace of God. (See Phil. 4:7.)

e) This is never a purely negative word. It never describes simply the absence of trouble. It describes the presence of serenity, trouble or not. It is a virtue quite independent of outward circumstances.

f) ILL: "God is love, regardless of which way the wind blows."

g) One can live in luxury and comfort and yet have no peace. One can live in poverty and privation, even a living hell, and have perfect peace.

CONCL: Now look at grace's supreme source: "from God our Father, and from the Lord Jesus Christ" (v. 2). God is the sovereign source of all blessings. Christ is the mediator and dispenser of those blessings. There is an admission to sonship, for He is "our Father." There is submission to Lordship, for Christ is "the Lord."

II. PRAISE FOR GOD'S PLAN

"Blessed be the God and Father of our Lord Jesus Christ, who hath blessed us with all spiritual blessings in heavenly places in Christ" (1:3).

Ephesians 1:3

INTRO: This is a great verse. It is the text of Ephesians. It is the key verse of the book because it contains in brief all that the entire epistle explains in detail. It is the central verse from which all the great spiritual truths in Ephesians flow.

Paul frequently capsules the whole gospel in just a brief phrase or a verse. This could easily be one of his most glorious capsules of truth. However, it is possible to get so charmed and enraptured by the words that you miss the deep richness of its content.

In the two-verse salutation, Paul reminds believers: Who they are: "the saints" and "the faithful," the best people in the world; What they are: "in Christ," the highest privilege in the world; What they have: "grace" and "peace" "from God our Father and from the Lord Jesus Christ," the choicest blessings in the world. Having explained that they are "saints," are "faithful," and are "in Christ," and as such, they now possess "grace" and "peace" from Christ, now in v. 3 he proceeds to show how all this is possible. The Spirit of God is upon Paul. He has just received the revelation of some rich and glorious spiritual truths. Upon the revelation of these great truths, the writer bursts forth in praise to God for His blessings.

Two great principles of the blessings of praise are stated here:

A. Praise is Natural to a Christian! (v. 3a)

1. True Salvation Always Leads to Praise. "Blessed" Gr: "eulogize, speak well of."

a) The knowledge of Christ and His saving grace always leads to heartfelt praise and adoration in worship.

b) It bursts forth here in the very first word, "blessed."

c) He starts most of his writings this way, "Blessed by God."

d) As the Spirit anoints him to pen great spiritual truths, he first breaks out in acclamation, "Blessed be God."

e) Praise and thanksgiving are and will ever be the one great characteristic of the Christian life.

f) The spirit of praise fairly characterized the NT church. Open the Book anywhere and praise leaps out at you, "Blessed."

g) After the ascension of Jesus, they returned to Jerusalem with great joy, and "were continually in the temple, praising and blessing God" (Luke 24:53).

h) During a praise meeting in the Upper Room, the Holy Ghost came upon them and gave them a more adequate language to praise and bless God with (see Acts 2).

i) At the healing of the cripple, he was "walking, and leaping, and praising God" (Acts 3:8).

j) The Redeemed of the Ages are round the throne of God in eternity, "saying, Amen: Blessing, and glory, and wisdom, and thanksgiving and honour, and power, and might, be unto our God forever and ever" (Rev. 7:12).

k) Praise and adoration are the highest forms of worship to Almighty God. Praise is the highest point one can reach in prayer. Praise is the main object of all public acts of worship.

2. Praise is Trinitarian in Character.

   a) This acclamation of praise and worship is ascribed to the Blessed Trinity.

   b) Praise to God, the source of our spiritual blessings. Praise to the Lord Jesus Christ, the Mediator of our spiritual blessings. Praise to the Holy Spirit, the agent of our spiritual blessings.

   c) The evangelical faith is trinitarian in its worship.

B. Praise is Reasonable to a Christian! (v. 3b)

1. There are two good reasons given here for praise:

    a) Praise God for Who He Is!

    b) We praise God for WHAT He does. More importantly, we praise God for WHO He is. Because HE is the Almighty God. Because of His mighty works, WHO HE IS and WHAT HE DOES are closely related.

        1) "The God and Father of our Lord Jesus Christ": This is an NT description of God. In the OT God is described as "the God of Abraham, Isaac, and Jacob"; "the God of Israel."

        2) The God of Abraham gave a Covenant. The God of Moses gave a Law. But to us, "the God and Father of our Lord Jesus Christ": "For God so loved the world, that he gave his only begotten son, that whosoever believeth in him should not perish, but have everlasting life" (John 3:16).

        3) God before time, before the world knew our sinful predicament, entered into a Covenant of Grace with His own Son on our behalf. He took an oath. He signed. He pledged Himself in a Covenant. He has committed Himself. Everything is in Christ. He is our Representative, Mediator, Guarantor. All blessings come through Him.

2. ILL: Someone may ask, "Have you received the second blessings?" Second blessing. I have not only had the second blessing, I have had thousands of blessings. "Blessed" Gr: "beneficent, to do well by."

3. God has blessed us in three ways:

    a) He Has Blessed Us "in all spiritual blessings" (v. 3).

        1) "Spiritual blessings"

        2) Gr: "All the blessings of the Spirit, referring to the Holy Spirit."

3) These are spiritual blessings as opposed to material: Grace. Salvation. Redemption. Peace. Joy. Forgiveness.

4) ILL: In OT God promised Israel material blessings as the reward for their obedience (see Deut. 28:1–13).

5) Today, He promises to supply all our needs (see Phil. 4:19).

6) They are complete—"all." Not SOME, but ALL. Temporal blessings are usually partial. Wealth without health. Conversely health without wealth. Spiritual blessings are always complete, fulfilling, and satisfying.

b) He Has Blessed Us "in heavenly *places*" (emphasis added) TR: "in the heavenlies."

1) It is speaking of that spiritual realm beyond the world perceived by senses. Where God dwells. Otherworldly.

2) Things that come from heaven and prepare us for heaven.

3) The unsaved are interested primarily in "earthlies" because this is where they live. Jesus called them (in Luke 16:8) "the children of this world."

4) The Christian's life is centered in Heaven. His citizenship is in Heaven (see Phil. 3:20). His name is written in Heaven (see Luke 10:20). His Father is in Heaven (see Matt. 6:9; Col. 3:2).

c) He Has Blessed Us "in Christ."

  1) Everything is in Him. All blessings come through Him. The phrase "in Christ" is repeated throughout this epistle 130 times. It is one of the truly spiritual NT statements.

  2) It means that a Christian not only believes in Christ, he is in a real sense "in Christ." He belongs to Him. He is united with Him. He is joined to Him.

  3) ILL: When the church is illustrated as a human body, believers are individual members of that Body (see 1 Cor. 12:12, 27).

  4) ILL: The same idea is presented in the analogy of Adam and Christ. (See 1 Cor. 15:22.)

      a. It says we were all originally in Adam. Adam was the first man and as such was representative of the entire human race. Everyone who has been born into this world was in Adam. A part of Adam. Joined to Adam.

      b. As we were all "in Adam" so now we who are Christian are "in Christ." As "in Adam" so "in Christ."

  5) What a tremendous, staggering truth. I am a part of Christ. I belong to Him. I am a member of the Body of Christ. I am not my own. I am in Christ. He is the Head. I am a member.

  6) There is a vital, organic, mystical union between us. Jesus said, "Abide in me, and I in you" (John 15:4). What a glorious, wonderful truth. Christ in me. I am in Christ.

      a. ILL: The bird is in the air; the air is in the bird. The fish is in the water; the water is in the fish. The iron is in the fire; the fire is in the iron.

      b. All God's blessings come to us because we are in Christ. No wonder Jesus said he is the vine and we are the branches. (See John 15:5.)

CONCL: The blessings of praise. When God blesses us, it's just MASAMARTL, natural to praise. We praise Him for His great blessings.

The more we are blessed, the more we praise. The more we praise, the more we are blessed. We just naturally praise God! Why is that so? Because: He has blessed us! He has blessed us *with spiritual blessings*! He has blessed us with *all* spiritual blessings! with all spiritual blessings *in heavenly places*! with all spiritual blessings in heavenly places *in Christ*!

ILL: There is a parallel here with God's people Israel. God had given them Canaan. He had blessed them with Canaan. (See Josh. 1:3.) They did not possess their possessions. Fear and unbelief kept them from crossing Jordan to enter. So for 40 years they wandered in the wilderness. Making no progress toward the promise, just going in circles. Are you possessing your blessings in Christ? What about salvation, justification, sanctification, Holy Spirit baptism, gifts, joy, peace, hope, contentment, fulfillment? You can stop going in circles and make progress toward the blessings that are yours in Christ.

III. GOD'S PURPOSE FOR YOU

*"According as he hath chosen us in him before the
foundation of the world, that we should be holy
and without blame before him in love" (1:4).*

Ephesians 1:4–6

INTRO: Paul was convinced God had a plan for his life! Are you? (See Jer. 1:5.) Paul knew God had a purpose for his life before birth. (See Gal. 1:15.) The Damascus Road experience was part of the working of God's purpose in his life. There the Spirit revealed that God had chosen him. (See Acts 22:14–15.)

The Divine Purpose which shaped Paul's life was a part of a larger purpose that includes all humanity and, in fact, embraces the whole creation. The Eternal Purpose of God is that in Christ all divided humanity should be united and gathered together into one body, the church. Christ is the Divine Agent for the consummation of that plan. The church is the dynamic center, the sign of hope that the work of redemption, which will ultimately unite all things, has begun.

Ephesians 1 forms an almost continuous prayer. Here Paul is not before a crowd proclaiming the truth. He is not behind a desk writing a reasoned statement of doctrine. He is on his knees in prayer. He breaks out into joyful praise for God's Plan (vv. 3–14). Then moves into deep intercession for God's people (vv. 15–23).

The prayer of praise (vv. 3–14) is one sentence in the original manuscript. One long, compound, complex, complicated sentence. It is not a reasoned statement of doctrine. But a joyful doxology of praise. Paul seems to write continuously as the Holy Spirit continues to reveal gift after gift, wonder after wonder: he cannot close the sentence. So this beautiful doxology of praise runs on and on in one grand sentence extolling the Eternal Purpose of God.

The gathering together in Christ of fragmented humanity into one body, the church. And ultimately, all things, the whole creation, the entire cosmos.

Paul makes three affirmations here that show how God is working out His Eternal Plan. This passage shows the work of the Father in planning our salvation. He has "chosen us"; "predestined us"; "accepted us."

A. God Has Chosen Us to be Saved in Christ (v. 4)

1. When chosen? "Before the foundation of the world."

    a) Paul, by the Spirit, is allowed a glimpse into the great eternity past. Somewhere, "before the foundation of the world," there is convened the Eternal Council of God: God—the Father, the Son, and the Holy Spirit.
    b) There the creation of man is decided (see Gen. 1:26).
    c) There the eternal plan of God is drawn up (v. 4). (See 1 Pet. 1:18–20; Rev. 13:8; 1 Pet. 1:2; Matt. 25:34.)

2. Who is chosen? "Us in him." Us believers. Those in Christ. It is the plan that is chosen for all believers, not each believer chosen, elected, and selected for the plan.

    a) ILL: Probably the only reason Paul speaks of election at all is to insist on the inclusion of the Gentile believers in God's Plan. Because the Jews insisted that they alone were God's elect, the chosen of God, for them alone the world was made. Ephesians corrects these prejudices.
    b) The NT doctrine of election allows "whosoever." (See Rev. 22:17; John 3:16; Rom. 10:13; 2 Pet. 3:9.)
    c) ILL: In regards to salvation: God is for us; Satan is against us; man breaks the tie!
    d) Who are the elect? Whosoever will! Whosoever believes! Whosoever calls! Whosoever comes to Christ!

3. What is chosen? "That we should be holy and without blame before him in love."

    a) Two purposes:

        1) "Holy" HAGIOS Gr: idea of difference, separation; God chose that His people should be different from other men.

2) To be "in" but not "of" the world. "Blameless" Gr: AMOMOS: idea is sacrificial. The Jewish Law required inspection of the sacrifice. No blemishes allowed. Only the best is fit to be offered to God. No second best accepted. God chose the best for His children, no blemishes allowed.

b) Two qualifications:

1) "Before Him." Not necessarily men, or even the church community.
2) "In love." Holiness profession or pretense w/o love is nothing. Like tongues, gifts, charity, or martyrdom.

B. God Has Predestined Us to Sonship by Adoption (v. 5)

1. Predestined to Adoption

   a) The Father has predestined us to the place of sonship by adoption. Predestined all believers to adoption into the family of God as children. But who becomes a believer is left to individual choice, his free will. The plan is predestined but not individual conformity to the plan.

   b) All believers are adopted into the family of God as children. (See John 1:12; Rom. 8:14; 2 Cor. 6:18; Gal. 4:5.) Jesus Christ is the only "begotten" Son of God. We are the "adopted sons of God. "Predestination" Gr: PROORISOS "to define, to mark out, to set apart, to horizon."

   c) ILL: If you go outside and look around, especially in a flat country, you can only see the horizon. You are "horizoned." You are put in that area. Predestination is never used in reference to the unsaved. God has never predestined anybody to be lost. You are lost by choice. Predestination refers only to those who are saved.

2. Predestined to Christlikeness (see Rom. 8:28–30)

   a) Those who love God, called according to His purpose, are predestined to be conformed to the image of His Son.

   b) Adoption means that we are brought into the place of full-grown sons.

C. God Has Made Us Accepted in the Beloved (v. 6)

1. "Made us accepted"

   a) For the purpose of God's glory. All to the praise of His glory. The work of our salvation and our adoption is done "to the praise of the glory of his grace."

   b) On the basis of God's grace: "made us accepted"; literally: "en-graced us," brought us into grace, or "be-graced us," bestowed Divine favor on us in the beloved; graced us with His grace.

   c) "In the Beloved." Who is it? It is the Lord Jesus Christ.

      1) At His Water Baptism. (See Matt. 3:17.)
      2) At His Transfiguration. (See Matt. 17:5.)

2. Additional Scripture References

   a) See John 17:24. God sees the believer, accepts the believer as He did His own Son. Only on that basis will I be in heaven. I am accepted in The Beloved. Just as God loves Christ, He loves me because I am in Christ.

   b) See John 17:23. We cannot make ourselves acceptable to God. God by His grace has made us accepted in Christ.

      1) Because of God's grace in Christ, we are accepted before Him.
      2) ILL: Like Paul wrote Philemon to accept Onesimus, the runaway slave, on the same basis. (See Philem. 17–19.)
      3) ILL: "Near, so very near to God, Nearer I could not be; For in the person of His Son, I'm just as near as He. Dear, so very dear to God, Dearer I could not be; For in the person of His Son, I'm just as dear as He."[1]

CONCL: So in God's Eternal Plan of Redemption: He has chosen us; He has adopted us; and He has accepted us.

---

1   Catesby Paget, "Near, so very near to God."

IV. CHRIST'S PROVISION FOR YOU

"In whom we have redemption through his blood, the forgiveness of sins, according to the riches of his grace" (1:7).

Ephesians 1:7–12

INTRO: This chapter contains some of the deepest doctrine to be found anywhere in Scripture. We have just been given the great picture of God's ultimate purpose and eternal plan for us. Three wonders. We are *made to wonder* that God has "chosen us" to be saved in Christ (v. 4). We are *given a glance* at our exalted position of sonship to which God has "predestinated us" (v. 5). We are *overwhelmed* that God has "made us accepted" in the Beloved (v. 6). This raises us to a position that requires us to be holy, without blame, without blemish, and without spot in the very presence of God.

So sinful may well raise a protest. "But we are still on earth, still fallible, still sinful." The question arises, how can we ever be brought into such an exalted relationship with God? Something must be done for that to happen. The great obstacle to our ever getting there is the obstacle of sin: *sin in general* and *sins in particular*. It is our sins that have separated us from God (see Isa. 59:1–2). So before we could ever realize God's purpose and plan for us, something had to be done about the problem of sin. To accomplish this special work of redemption, the Son of God came into the world. God devised a way whereby sinful man could be reconciled to God. And the way is given here. The obstacle has been removed. The problem has been solved.

Here is a concise summary of the whole content of the gospel. When the Son of God stepped down from eternity into time and space with the blueprints of the church, God's Plan of Redemption in His hands, the History of Time was split into a *before* and *after*.

The *historical facts* are that God was incarnate when Jesus was born of a virgin. That the Son of God tabernacled among men and lived virtuously on earth 33 years. That Christ died a vicarious death for our sins on the cross. That Christ rose again victorious over death, hell, and the grave and ascended triumphantly to heaven to appear in God's presence for us. That Christ will return visibly in glory to this earth for His own.

This passage shows the work of the Son in accomplishing our salvation. It makes a magnificent statement concerning Christ's accomplishments in providing for our salvation.

A. Christ Has Redeemed Us Through His Blood (v. 7)

Note two words found in two phrases:

1. The REDEMPTION Through His Blood!

   a) "In whom" refers to the Beloved, Christ our Lord and Savior. Redemption is the primary work of Christ.

   b) LIT: "In Whom we have THE redemption." In OT it was a redemption. In NT it is THE redemption. Ultimate, final redemption. This is the reason Christ came to earth. To pay the price for our redemption. (See Matt. 20:28.)

   c) There are three Greek words translated "redemption" in the NT.

      1) Gr: AGORAZO means "to buy at the marketplace." The idea is to buy as one's own possession. The emphasis is on the price and ownership. (See 1 Cor. 6:20.)

      2) Gr: EXAGORAZO means "to buy out of the marketplace." The thought is buying something for one's own use. Not to resell for profit, but to keep for one's own use. (See Gal. 3:13.)

      3) Gr: APOLUTROSIS (used in v. 7) means "To liberate by the paying of a ransom in order to set a person free." The idea is buying a slave out of slavery in order to set him free. Man is sold under sin and is in bondage to the slavery of sin. (See John 8:36.)

   d) "Through His blood" was the price which He paid. Sin carried the death penalty. The ransom price was blood. (See Heb. 9:22; 1 Pet. 1:18–19.)

2. The FORGIVENESS of Sins!

    a) Human forgiveness and Divine forgiveness are not the same.

        1) Human forgiveness is always based on the fact that a penalty is deserved and that the penalty is suspended and not imposed.

        2) God is holy and righteous; therefore Divine forgiveness is always based on the fact that *there has been the execution of the penalty and the price has been paid.*

        3) Human forgiveness comes before the penalty is executed. Overlooking the wrong.

        4) Divine forgiveness depends upon the penalty being executed. Correcting the wrong.

    b) The righteousness of the law demands that the penalty must be paid.

        1) The penalty was paid for sin when Christ died for our sins on the cross. Forgiveness depends on the blood of Christ.

        2) The shedding of the blood of Christ at His death on the cross is the foundation for the forgiveness of sins.

        3) God could not forgive until the penalty had been paid.

    c) All this, redemption and forgiveness, "according to [not out of] the riches of his grace."

B. Christ Has Revealed in Us the Mystery of His Will (vv. 8–10)

1. The Gifts of His Grace

    a) Wisdom and Prudence! V. 8: "Wherein" refers to the riches of His grace. From the riches of His grace we are given a plenteous supply of wisdom and prudence. "Abounded" Gr: "lavished, overflowed, overabundance; overflowed into our lives a plenteous supply."

        1) "Wisdom" Gr: SOPHIA "spiritual wisdom, knowledge of the most precious things in life, solution to the eternal

problems of life: God and man; life and death; time and eternity."

   2) "Prudence" Gr: PHRONESIS "natural discernment, knowledge of human affairs, things in which planning is necessary, common sense to meet and solve the practical problems of everyday life and living."

b) From the riches of His grace we have a plenteous supply of intellectual knowledge, which solves life's great mysteries, and practical knowledge, common sense, which handles life's everyday problems.

2. The Mystery of His Will: Christ and the Church! (vv. 9–10) "Mystery"—Not mystic or unknowable; refers to the heretofore hidden will of God now revealed in the gospel. "Dispensation of the fulness of times"—The goal of history. God's plan for the ages.

a) Christ: All things reunited in Christ. Christ is the Divine Agent for the consummation of God's plan.

b) The Church: All men gathered together in one body. The church is the Dynamic Center for the consummation of the eternal plan of redemption. Unity is God's Purpose for created order. The purpose of the church is the gathering into one all-divided, polarized, separated humanity. The existence of the church is a sign that the plan of redemption has begun. This truth was concealed in the OT and revealed in the NT.

C. Christ Has Rewarded Us with His Inheritance (vv. 11–12)

1. We Have Obtained An Inheritance!

a) God gives us an inheritance. He rewards us for something we have not done. God's purpose is that believers should have a part in Christ's inheritance. (See Rom. 8:17.)

b) Here is another marvelous truth: All things are ours. (See 1 Cor. 3:21–23.) A powerful, all-encompassing statement.

2. To The Praise Of His Glory!

   a) God does not exist to satisfy every whim and wish of believers. Conversely, the believer exists for the glory of God.

   b) God will be able throughout the endless ages of eternity to point to you and me and say, "Look at them; they were not worth saving, but I loved them and I saved them."

   c) That alone gives worth, standing, dignity, purpose, joy, and glory to life. We exist today to the praise of his glory; that is enough.

CONCL: This passage on the Son's provision for our salvation closes with two appropriate references. The beginning and the ending of our salvation: (1) The coming of Christ and our inheritance with Him. (2) Our trust in Christ. You can trust the One who died for you!

Real faith is more than believing, it is trusting! Believing can be just a mental assent to the truth. But the idea of trust denotes personal involvement. It assumes a relationship of some sort between the one expressing trust and the person or thing being trusted.

ILL: The difference between belief and trust is the difference between acknowledging that a bridge is capable of holding a person's weight, and actually walking out on the bridge. One is just acknowledgment, but the other is actual dependence.

ILL: D. L. Moody used to say, "You can travel first class or second class to Heaven. Second Class is 'What time I am afraid, I will trust' [Ps. 56:3]. First Class is 'I will trust, and not be afraid' [Isa. 12:2]. That is the better way. Why not buy a First Class ticket?"

FORGIVENESS: See 1 John 1:9. Forgiveness is available only to those who put personal trust in Christ. Christ provided forgiveness, but it must be appropriated on a personal basis. Although provided for by Christ, it has no effect on the sin debt of the person who has not personally put trust in Christ.

ILL: It is like a paycheck that is never picked up. It is like a gift certificate that is never redeemed. It is like a lifeline that is ignored by a drowning man.

BLOOD: There are 290 references to the love of God in the NT, 290 times when God declares His love for mankind. In the same NT there are 1,300-plus references to atonement, 1,300 assurances that salvation is through the blood of Christ.

ILL: A preacher was speaking from the text 1 John 1:17. Suddenly he was interrupted by an atheist saying, "How can blood cleanse sin?" After a momentary silence, the preacher replied, "How can water quench thirst?" Infidel replied, "I don't know, but I know it does." Preacher followed, "Neither do I know how the blood of Jesus cleanses sin, but I know it does." (See 1 Cor. 3:21–23.)

V. THE HOLY SPIRIT'S POWER IN YOU

*"Ye were sealed with the Holy Spirit of promise, Which
is the earnest of our inheritance." (1:13b–14a)*

Ephesians 1:13–14

INTRO: In Ephesians 1 we find the greatest news story to ever break upon this old sinful earth. It is *the story of God's Redeeming Love*. It traces the plan of salvation that began in the mind of God even before the foundation of the world and will continue on into eternity future.

This grand story of redemption is related here in three progressions: Beginning *from eternity past* where we see the *work of the Father in planning* our salvation (vv. 4–6). Progressing on *into history past* where we see *the work of the Son in accomplishing* our redemption (vv. 7–12). Now we *arrive at the immediate day of grace* where we see *the work of the Holy Spirit in applying* our salvation (vv. 13–14).

The great plan of salvation was *thought by the Father, bought by the Son*, and is now being *wrought by the Spirit*. The application of Christ's work of redemption at Calvary is the work of the Holy Spirit. He is at work applying salvation individually to each believer. His work within us relating to salvation is twofold. Here the twofold work of the Holy Spirit in salvation is explained by two common illustrations. The sealing and the earnest. One has to do with the *beginning of our salvation*. The other deals with the *completion of our salvation*.

A. The Sealing of the Spirit (v. 13)

Now we go from Christ's work for us to the Holy Spirit's work in us. Christ's provision. Spirit's application. Our appropriation.

1. The Holy Spirit's first demonstration of power in us is the power to save. This scripture does not refer to the baptism of the Spirit, the enduement of power for service.
2. It speaks of the ministry of the HS in the work of regeneration, the experience of salvation. While this verse does not specify

regeneration, it shows in a marvelous way the Ephesians' experience of salvation.

3. Four things are said about their salvation experience.

    a) Ye Heard – The Gospel of Your Salvation!" The hearing of the Word preached by the anointing of the Spirit is the first step to salvation. (See Rom. 10:13–14, 17; Titus 1:3; 1 Cor. 1:31.) The HS convicts the heart of the unbeliever through the preached word that he is lost and needs salvation.

    b) "Ye Believed – The Word of Truth!" The HS convinces the mind of the unbeliever that God has provided for his salvation and can save him. (See John 1:12; Rom. 10:9–10.)

    c) "Ye Trusted in Christ!" The HS converts or changes the heart and life of the believer. Hearing is first, believing follows, and trusting is the final step to salvation. At the moment a person trusts Christ for the forgiveness of sins and takes Him as Savior, he is saved. Believe and trust are different. Believe can be of the head. Trust is always of the heart. F - A - I - T - H: For All I Trust Him. Forsaking All I Take Him.

    d) "Ye Were Sealed - With The Spirit!" At the moment we trust Christ, we are sealed by the HS. (See Rom. 8:16; Gal. 4:6; Rom. 8:9; 1 Cor. 12:13.) The HS is the agent of our salvation. He convinces men of truth. He convicts men of sin. He draws men to Christ. They are born of the Spirit. He witnesses that they are children of God. They who are Christ's have the Spirit of Christ. The Spirit baptizes them into one body. The Spirit resides in them.

        1) The sealing of which Paul speaks refers to an official mark of identification that was placed on a letter, contract, or other important documents.

        2) The seal usually was made of hot wax, which was placed on the document and then impressed (imprinted) with a signet ring.

        3) When the HS seals believers:

            a. It establishes authenticity! (See Rom. 8:16.)

        b. The HS makes our profession authentic. Christ's image is stamped within us. (See Rom. 8:29.) The imprint reads, "This person belongs to Christ and is an authentic citizen of my Kingdom and member of my family."

        c. The Spirit authenticates our salvation.

    4) ILL: See John 3:33; 6:27. God the Father authenticated the Son at His baptism with the Spirit in the form of a dove; at His transfiguration with his audible voice; with miracles, signs, and wonders.

4. It denotes ownership! (See Rom. 8:9.) They are marked as God's personal property. His own peculiar ("privately owned") people, who entirely belong to Him.

B. The Earnest of the Spirit (v. 14)

While the sealing authenticates our present experience, the earnest guarantees what is sure to come, our future prospects. Interestingly, sealing/earnest are often linked. (See 2 Cor. 1:21–22.)

1. The Earnest of Our Inheritance! "Earnest" Gr: ARRABON originally referred to a down payment or earnest money given to secure a purchase. Later it came to represent any sort of pledge or guarantee. A form of the word even came to be used for an engagement ring.

    a) What we have now is just partial payment or earnest, and this earnest guarantees the full delivery of our heavenly inheritance.

    b) Our redemption will not be complete until we are glorified.

    c) We now have justification, sanctification, but our redemption will not be complete until we experience glorification.

2. The Redemption of the Purchased Possession! Christ purchased us at Calvary. We are His property. (See 1 John 3:2; Rom. 8:19, 22–23.)

a) The final stage of our redemption is possession of glorification.
b) Redemption will not be complete until Jesus returns in glory.
c) He came the first time to take the world out of us. The second time to take us out of the world.
d) The first, to redeem our soul. The second, to redeem our body.
e) The first, He made us a new creature. The second, He will give us a new body.

CONCL: The Ephesians understood perfectly the figures of the seal and the earnest. Ephesus was a seaport carrying on an extensive lumber business. The lumber merchant came to Ephesus and purchased his timber. He left an earnest of money to guarantee his return to claim his possession. He stamped or sealed it with the acknowledged sign of ownership, his signet. Oftentimes he left his purchase in the harbor with other floats. Sometime later he sent a trusted agent, who compared the imprint of the signet and took away the lumber belonging to his employer/master.

The Holy Spirit is the signet seal of ownership which God places in each believer. He is the Divine Imprint of identification and the guarantee of His return to redeem the purchased possession, and of our everlasting inheritance. (See 2 Cor. 5:1–5.)

ILL: Spirit of Expectation (vv. 13–14). There is an inscription in the dome of our capitol in Washington which few people know about. It says, "One far-off divine event toward which the whole creation moves." A visitor saw this inscription and asked the guide what it meant. He said: "I think it refers to the second coming of Christ." When the dome of our capitol was erected, some God-fearing official ordered that inscription to be etched in the dome of our seat of government, believing its truth was of vital concern to our nation.

VI. THE PRAISE OF HIS GLORY

*"To the praise of the glory of his grace, wherein he
hath made us accepted in the beloved." (1:6)*

Ephesians 1:6, 12, 14

INTRO: This is a glorious phrase revealing the ultimate purpose of the plan of redemption. It is uniquely positioned throughout this chapter. Let me show you.

After the work of God the Father (vv. 1–6), back in eternity past before the foundation of the world, designing the plan of salvation. Where we were: chosen to be holy, predestined to sonship, and well-favored in the Beloved. The HS adds divine purpose to it all (v. 6), "to the praise of the glory of his grace."

After the work of God the Son (vv. 7–12) in history passed on the cross of Calvary, accomplishing the plan of salvation. There we were: redeemed by His blood, made a part of His church, and given an eternal inheritance. The HS adds divine purpose to it all (v. 12), "that we should be to the praise of his glory."

While the Holy Spirit is at work (vv. 13–14) in the immediate present day of grace, applying the plan of salvation. Convicting of sin. Convincing of truth. Converting the sinner. Cleansing the believer. The inspired Word adds divine purpose to it all (v. 14).

The great plan of redemption has three grand parts for the good of man and to the glory of God. They are salvation, sanctification, and glorification.

This phrase relates to and gives meaning to each. When we experience salvation, forgiveness of sins, and are made accepted in the beloved. It is "to the praise of the glory of his grace" (v. 6). Glory of a changed heart. When we experience sanctification, after we trust Christ. It is "that we should be to the praise of his glory" (v. 12)! The glory of a clean life. When we experience glorification at the redemption of the purchased possession as we are guaranteed by the earnestness of our inheritance. It is "unto the praise of his glory" (v. 14).

This phrase seems to naturally divide into two streams of glory:

A. The Glory of God

1. God's glory is impossible to describe because our language, terminology, and words are inadequate to convey any true sense of it.

2. But we can say the glory of God is the essential nature of God. It is that which makes God God. It is the Presence of God, the very essence of God, the light of God. (See Heb. 1:3.) "Glory" describes God more fully than any other term. For it means "beauty, majesty, splendor." It includes the idea of "greatness, might, and eternity." All of this and more is included in this word "glory."

3. It is the highest form of existence in the universe. You cannot go beyond it.

4. This resplendent radiance is suggested in the expression. (See 1 John 1:5.)

5. Look at some of the examples of the manifestation of God's Glory:

    a) Old Testament manifestations of God's Glory!

        1) It was the Shekinah Glory of God that stood above the mercy seat between the two golden cherubim in the Holy of Holies of the OT Tabernacle.

        2) It was the Glory of God in the cloud that filled the Temple so the priests could not stand to minister.

        3) It was the Glory of God that flashed in the lightning and blazed in the devouring fire atop Mt. Sinai when Moses received the Ten Commandments. (Also Moses's face had to be veiled.)

        4) It was the Glory of God that burned in the unconsumed bush at Mt. Horeb when Moses was called to deliver Israel.

    5) It was the brightness of the Glory of God that stood between the armies of Egypt and the children of Israel at the Red Sea.

    6) It was the Glory of God that blazed in the pillar of fire that led Israel by night out of Egypt's bondage.

    7) It was the Glory of God that illuminated the cloud that led Israel by day toward God's promised land. (See Ex. 33:18–23; Lev. 9:22–24.)

  b) New Testament manifestations of God's Glory! (See Heb. 1:1–3; John 1:51.) Jesus was not only the "express image" of the person of God, but also "the brightness" and "the effulgence of" the glory of God (Heb. 1:3; Heb. 1:3 ASV).

    1) It was the Glory of God that shone round about the Judean shepherds when the angels announced Christ's birth.

    2) It was the Glory of God that blazed from the star which led the wise men to the place where the Christ child lay.

    3) It was the Glory of God that radiated through Jesus's countenance and robe at His transfiguration.

    4) It was the Glory of God that came down in the Upper Room in the form of a rushing, mighty wind and tongues of fire.

    5) It was the Glory of God that Paul described at his conversion on the Damascus Road above the brightness of the noonday sun.

    6) It was the Glory of God that gave dying Stephen the countenance of an angel at his trial and execution.

    7) It was the Glory of God that John the Revelator saw in that indescribable vision on the Isle of Patmos.

B. **The Glory of Grace (vv. 6, 12, 14)**

1. This transcendent Glory of God is generally associated with the conception of our salvation.

   a) ILL: In the OT Tabernacle, which is only a pale copy of the truth, the Shekinah Glory of God was located between the cherubim above the mercy seat in the Holy of Holies. Here mercy and glory are side by side.

   b) ILL: Before sin, God in all His glory came down, walked, and communed with Adam in the cool of the day in Eden. But man rebelled and sinned against God. Then at the east end of the garden, God placed His Glory in cherubim and flaming sword to prevent man from returning to Paradise and the Tree of Life.

   c) The most Biblical and spiritual definition of sin: see Rom. 3:23.

2. The Glory of God is uniquely revealed in our salvation.

   a) When the Angelic Choir announced Christ's birth and God's Glory shone round about them. (See Luke 1:11, 14.) The moment salvation is mentioned, the Glory of God is most prominent.

   b) Paul informed Timothy that what had been committed to him was "the gospel of the glory of the blessed God" (1 Tim. 11:1 ASV). (See 2 Cor. 4:6; John 1:14.)

   c) Our salvation is the highest manifestation of God's Glory.

      1) The Glory of God is revealed in nature! (See Ps. 91:1.)

      2) The Glory of God is revealed in history!

      3) The Glory of God is revealed in His holiness and His Righteousness! (See Rom. 3:25; Matt. 5:16.)

3. The Glory of God is ultimately revealed in our glorification.

   a) This will be ours at the coming of the Lord. The rapture of the saints. The redemption of the purchased possession. The earnestness guarantees the completion of our redemption. (See Col. 1:27.)

b) We now have justification, and our glorification is guaranteed. We are partakers of grace. We are to partake of glory. (See John 17:22, 24; 2 Cor. 5:1; 1 Cor. 15:49–53; Rom. 8:30; 1 Pet. 5:1; Col. 3:4; 1 John 3:2; Phil. 13:21.)

CONCL: God has initiated the great plan of salvation (v. 5). We did not deserve it nor desire it. Wholly of God. "Praise" Gr: EPAINOS "to extol, to glorify, to magnify, to approve, to commend, to eulogize, to acclaim, to honor, to laud." We now enjoy His grace in which we glorify Him. The ultimate praise of God's glory is our glorification.

ILL: A prosperous man lay dying. His lawyer was at his side settling his estate affairs. His little daughter, playing nearby, had heard the adult conversation about the legal matters. She gathered that her father was going to leave the house in which he lived and that it was to be passed on to someone else. With all a child's simplicity, "Father, when you leave this house, where are you going to live?" A good question. A sensible question. All should answer.

VII. PRAYER FOR GOD'S PEOPLE

"The eyes of your understanding being enlightened; that
ye may know what is the hope of his calling, and what the
riches of the glory of his inheritance in the saints." (1:18)

Ephesians 1:15–23

INTRO: This is one of the prayers of Paul. A profitable study. There are four such prayers in Paul's Epistles, two of which are in Ephesians. In ch. 3 he prays for enablement—strength to live! In ch. 1 he prays for enlightenment—light to know! It is a prayer for spiritual enlightenment, comprehension of the believer.

In the classic doxology of praise (vv. 1–14), the Christian's position is established:

- He is "blessed" in Christ! (v. 3)

- He is "chosen" to holiness! (v. 4)

- He is "predestined" to sonship! (v. 5)

- He is "accepted" by grace! (v. 6)

- He is "forgiven" of sins! (v. 7)

- He is "enlightened" to live! (v. 8)

- He has "obtained" an inheritance! (v. 11)

- He is "sealed" by the Holy Spirit! (v. 13)

Having viewed his position, now he prays for perception (vv. 15–23). He engages in two forms of prayer: thanksgiving and supplication. He begins with a prayer of thanks, "[I] cease not to give thanks for you." Thankful for two things: loyalty, "faith in the Lord Jesus"; and love, "love unto all the saints" (v. 15). He continues with a petition for perception. When Paul saw God's plan, the believers' position, he could not help but pray for spiritual perception, enlightenment—that they may comprehend God's plan, their position in it.

ILL: In any competitive sport, athletes are prone to gravitate to the part of the playing field where the action is. Opponent capitalizes on that tendency, runs a reverse play to gain or score. The coach screams at the players, "Play your position." Christian, know your place, position, and function there. Spiritually play your position. This prayer naturally divides itself into two parts: that God may give and that you may know.

VIII. THAT GOD MAY GIVE— SPIRITUAL PERCEPTION

*"That the God of our Lord Jesus Christ, the Father
of glory, may give unto you the spirit of wisdom and
revelation in the knowledge of him" (1:17).*

Ephesians 1:15–17

INTRO: Do you know God? Do you want to know God better? Some people are estranged from God. Feel guilty. They do not know Him as well as they know they should. Some people have superficial knowledge of God. They know the God of the church. But they do not know the God of NT.

This begins Paul's prayer for the spiritual perception of God's people. In the first half of this chapter, he has just closed the great doxology of praise, blessing God "who hath blessed us with all spiritual blessings in heavenly places" (v. 3). It includes a statement of God's Eternal Purpose of Redemption, Christ's provision for our salvation, and the Holy Spirit's power in saving us.

The gist of Paul's prayer is that the people may know this great-good God and understand His blessings to them.

However, many professed Christians do not perceive, nor fully comprehend, all their blessings. They have not appropriated all their provisions, nor possessed all their possessions. They simply do not know what is theirs.

ILL: I read the story of the late newspaper publisher William Randolph Hearst. He invested a fortune collecting art treasures from around the world. One day he discovered a description of some valuable pieces that he felt he must own. So he sent an agent abroad to find them. After scouring the great art galleries of the world, he finally found the treasures. They were in Mr. Hearst's warehouse! Hearst had been frantically searching for treasures he already owned. If he had had a knowledge of what was his, he could have saved himself a lot of trouble and expense.

Paul's concern here is that the Christians would know God better. These verses give us some powerful insights about the *people* of God and their *knowledge* of God.

A. The People of God (vv. 15–17a)

"Wherefore" LIT: "on this account." On account of God's revelation of His Glory and blessings to you (v. 16).

1. The People Who Need To Know! They were truly Christian and Paul thanks God for them. Here are given the two primary ways of validating a real Christian:

    a) Loyalty—"your faith in the Lord Jesus."

      1) "Your faith" Gr: "the down-among-you faith." Distributive sense.

      2) Not just speaking of the beginning of faith, a saving faith. It speaks of their living faith. The day-by-day faith exercised in the Lord Jesus for daily living. Not just Sunday faith, but everyday faith. It refers to both the saving faith by which they entered the Christian life and the living faith by which they continue to live the Christ life.

    b) Love—"your love unto all the saints."

      1) The second mark of genuine salvation is love for all the saints.

      2) "Agape love": Divine love in the heart. Not just human affections.

      3) Their love is indiscriminate for "all the saints." It does not pick and choose which believers it will love. Some assert, "I love him in the Lord." That seems to communicate, "I only love him spiritually because I have to, but I hate him naturally."

      4) Sadly, this sort of love did not last. Faith was kept true and pure. But God said, "Thou hast left thy first love" (Rev. 2:3).

c) Faith and love must be kept in balance. Monks and hermits make great effort to keep the faith but refuse to reach out to others in love. Unfortunately, some have a loveless kind of faith.

2. The God They Need To Know!

   He seems to remind himself of certain things about God before he utters a word of prayer. This reminder emphasizes two great attributes of the God we need to know.

   a) The Redeeming God—"the God of our Lord Jesus Christ."

      1) Under the first covenant in the OT, the prophets and people prayed to "the God of Abraham, Isaac, and Jacob." It reminded them of God's Covenant of Promise with Abraham.

      2) When Paul uses the phrase "the God of our Lord Jesus Christ," it reminds them of the new covenant, the Covenant of Grace. He reminds them that he is praying to the God of our salvation, the God who planned and provided redemption through Christ. The greatest knowledge of God is to know His redemptive nature.

   b) The Glorious God—"the Father of glory."

      1) It means that God is the source and embodiment of glory. He is the Father to whom glory belongs.

      2) The ultimate character of God is glory. He is the source of glory. He is the summation of all glory in Himself. He also gives glory. He is prepared to impart that glory to the Redeemed. He is our Father. A father gives. He gives glory. He manifests it. He imparts it.

B. The Knowledge of God (v. 1:17b)

1. This does not mean God's knowledge, a knowledge which belongs to God. It refers to our knowledge of God.
2. We can know God! That is the focal point of the new covenant prophesied by Jeremiah and quoted twice in Hebrews (chs. 8 and 10). (See Heb. 8:11.)
3. This knowledge is open to all and is God-given through the Holy Spirit.
4. Three important considerations here:

    a) The Spirit of Wisdom

    1) "Spirit" Gr: "wind, breath, air, spirit, attitude, disposition, influence." This is the key to the verse.
    2) "Wisdom" LIT: "knowledge, information, understanding."
    3) It carries the complex idea of the spirit of man dwelt in and moved on by the Spirit of God. It is the Holy Spirit working on the human spirit to produce an attitude concerned with understanding wisdom and revelation in the knowledge of Him. A God-given, Spirit-prompted attitude that hungers after the knowledge of God. A God-given, Spirit-prompted attitude, disposition, or influence of wisdom.

    b) The Spirit of Revelation

    1) "Revelation" Gr: denoting the capacity of comprehending the revealed; perceiving the meaning of what God makes known so that it is a real revelation to us.
    2) ILL: Simon Peter (See Matt. 16:17.)
    3) ILL: Spiritual things (See 1 Cor. 2:9–10.)

    c) The Knowledge of Him

    1) "Knowledge," a strong, powerful Gr. term. Not a casual acquaintance. Not superficial knowledge.
    2) Gr. carries the idea of "accurate, exact knowledge, certain knowledge, experiential, intimate knowledge."

3) It is the fullest knowledge we can think of. A full-orbed knowledge, accurate, precise, exact, experiential, intimate knowledge.

4) We are not talking about a general, intellectual, theoretical knowledge of God. Not speaking of the God of theology, the God of the textbook, the God of propositions, but the living God, the personal God. (See 2 Pet. 3:18; Eph. 3:17–19; Phil. 3:10.)

5) See also Col. 1:10 and 1 Cor. 2:1–16. This chapter is the best commentary on v. 17.

CONCL: How can I know God better? In the face of Jesus Christ! Through the power of the Holy Ghost! Through the revelation of the Word of God!

There is an oft-repeated and mostly misunderstood verse in Prov. 29:18: "Where there is no vision, the people perish." "Vision," LIT: A redemptive revelation of God in the spirit of man by the Word of God. It is seeing the God of the Bible by the illuminating power of the Holy Spirit.

Do you know God? This knowledge is open to all! It is not a matter of IQ; does not depend on circumstances and conditions.

There are only two things that determine your knowing God: The realization that it is possible, then the personal desire to know Him! You can know God! The sinner can know God as Savior and Lord. The saint can know God better in all His power and might! The infidel says there is no God to know. The agnostic says if there is a God, you cannot know Him. The apostle declares there is a glorious God, and you can know Him better through the illuminating power of the Holy Spirit.

ILL: I have enjoyed the Bible teaching of James Montgomery Boice on many occasions. This Presbyterian pastor confessed that a post-college group once shocked him with a question. "What do you think is the greatest lack among evangelical Christians in America today?" Many good answers: The three essentials to spiritual survival: personal prayer, Bible study, church attendance; dedication, commitment, righteousness. But from the heart came, "I think that the greatest need of the evangelical church today is for professing Christians really to know God."

IX. THAT YOU MAY KNOW— SPIRITUAL ENLIGHTENMENT

*"The eyes of your understanding being enlightened; that
ye may know what is the hope of his calling, and what the
riches of the glory of his inheritance in the saints" (1:18).*

Ephesians 1:18–23

INTRO: When Paul sees God's great master plan of the ages, he prays for the spiritual enlightenment of God's people.

ILL: All of us have seen a bewildered person trying ever so hard to grasp the meaning of a difficult idea-problem. One can almost see the mind working, wheels turning, levers clicking, and eyes studying. Then out of nowhere the light comes on, it dawns on him, and suddenly without notice the exasperated person exclaims, "Oh, now I see." He means, "Now, I understand—Now, I know." This is what Paul is praying for all believers. Spiritual Enlightenment.

ILL: Jesus spoke of some "having eyes" to see, they "see . . . not" (see Mark 8:18). Fish in the Mammoth Cave have been discovered to have eyes, but they cannot see. They have lived in darkness so long, and not being used, their eyes become sightless.

Phrase: "the eyes of your understanding being enlightened." This speaks of the eyes of the heart. "Understanding" Gr: KARDIA for heart, the inner man, the center of personality, the source of our being. "Enlightened" Gr: PHOTIZO "to shed rays, to shine, to brighten up, give light, make to see."

Phrase: "That ye may know." Some things God wants us to know. Heart knowledge, not head knowledge. Revealed, not acquired. If you have something and do not know about it, it is of no benefit to you.

ILL: "And God gave Solomon wisdom and understanding exceeding much, and largeness of heart" (1 Kings 4:29). Spiritual understanding has nothing to do with IQ; it has only to do with spiritual sensibility to the Holy Spirit.

ILL: "Having the understanding darkened, being alienated from the life of God through ignorance that is in them, because of the blindness of their heart" (4:18).

A prayer for *threefold spiritual realization in life*. Called the prayer for three WHATS: "WHAT is the hope of his calling, and WHAT are the riches of the glory of his inheritance in the saints, and WHAT is the exceeding greatness of his power to usward who believe." Three things God wants you to know:

A. What is the Hope of His Calling? (v. 18a)

1. A New Realization of the Christian Hope!
2. His Calling! This calling of God is not without context. God has called us to something and for something.
3. It is linked with God's purpose for us in the first half of this chapter. God has chosen us to be holy and blameless in His sight. God has predestined us to the position of sonship by adoption. God has blessed us with all spiritual blessings in heavenly places. God has called and chosen us "for the praise of His glory."
4. LIT: "the calling of His hope." The hope which he calls us to. In His calling there is hope: salvation, sanctification, justification, glorification. God called us to repentance; the hope is we can turn around! God called us from sin; the hope is we can get out of sin! God called us to righteousness; the hope is we can be righteous! God called us to eternal life; the hope is resurrection, immortality.

   a) High Calling (See Phil. 3:14.)
   b) Holy Calling (See 2 Tim. 1:9.)
   c) Heavenly Calling (See Heb. 3:1.)

5. The Hope! (See 1 Cor. 15:19.)

    a) We have hope in a hopeless world. In Christian circles, the worth of a man is determined not by his background (where he comes from) but by where he is going.

    b) In general usage, "hope" is used for uncertain things.

    c) In the Bible the word is used of that which is certain because it is grounded on what God has done for us in Christ.

        1) Living Hope (See 1 Pet. 1:3–5.)

        2) Blessed Hope (See Titus 2:13.)

        3) Purifying Hope (See 1 John 3:2–3.)

B. **What is the Riches of His Inheritance? (v. 18b)**

1. A New Realization of The Church's Heritage!

2. The calling of hope deals with assurance of His blessings. The riches of inheritance deals with scope of blessings.

3. It is the inheritance of both Christ and the saints.

    a) The Saints Have an Inheritance in Christ! Grace here; glory hereafter. Present grace; future glory.

    b) Three things we need to know:

        1) Know—"His inheritance"

        2) Know—"the glory of His inheritance"

        3) Know—"the riches of the glory of His inheritance."

            a. "Riches" recurring word in Ephesians: "the riches of His grace" (1:7); "who is rich in mercy" (2:4); "the unsearchable riches of Christ" (3:8); "grant you according to the riches of His glory" (3:16)

            b. Jesus: "The glory which thou gavest me I have given them" (John 17:22). Human glory is often unjustly accorded and quickly passes. But His glory is real and everlasting.

    c) Christ Also Has an Inheritance in the Saints! All that God gives us will ultimately be His on that glorious day of the consummation of all things.

        1) The saints are His highest possession—spiritual beings.

        2) The saints are His original possession—divine creation.

        3) The saints are His purchased possession—vicarious atonement.

        4) The saints are His inheritance: He will not forsake it; He will care for it; and He will claim it.

C. What is the Greatness of His Power? (vv. 19–23)

1. A New Realization of the Believer's Power!

   The greatness of His power is emphasized in two ways:

   a) A Stockpile of Power Words! (v. 19)

       1) DUNAMIS: "power"—His natural, inherent power

       2) ENERGEIA: "working"—His working, operative power

       3) KRATOS: "mighty"—His forceful, manifested power

       4) ISCHUOS: "power"—His strong, exertive power

   b) All modified by the superlative "exceeding greatness." Gr: HYPERBALLON, LIT: "a throwing beyond, surpassing." It speaks of power beyond measure, more than enough, surpassing greatness, immeasurable, and unlimited. TR: "And how vast the resources of His power open to us who believe, as seen in the working of His infinite might."

2. A Summation of Powerful Examples!

   a) His resurrection power (v. 20a)

       1) By which power Jesus was raised from the dead.

       2) By which power we are raised from the deadness of sin to walk in newness of life. (See Col. 2:12; 1:29; Eph. 3:20.)

        a. The great power that broke the bonds of death can break the chains of sin.

        b. The great power that raised the dead can raise the sick.

        c. The great power that restored life can restore our joy.

  b) His intercessory power (v. 20b)

      1) By which power Christ ascended to the Father's right hand.

      2) By which power He supplies all our needs according to His riches in glory.

      3) From that powerful position in the heavenlies, He ever lives to make intercession for us. (See Rom. 8:34.)

      4) See Heb. 7:25. Gr: SOZO-to deliver, protect, do well by

  c) His sovereign power (vv. 21–23)

      1) By which power Christ is exalted above all.

      2) Not just "above" but "far above." How far is far? Far is too far to know how far far is.

      3) Not just above some or most, but "above all."

        a. Above all Angels—fallen or unfallen.

        b. Above every name—earthly or heavenly.

        c. Above all things—present or future.

        d. Head over the church—militant or triumphant.

      4) By which power He reigns as Lord of All! Lord of Lords! King of Kings!

3. What Powerful Preeminence!

  a) Above all principality.

  b) Above all power.

  c) Above all might.

  d) Above all dominion.

  e) Above every name that is named.

  f) Above every name in this world.

g) Above every name in the world to come.
h) Head over all things in the world.
i) Head over all things to the church.
j) "The fullness of Him that filleth all in all."

CONCL: Oh the greatness of His purpose, power, and person.
Do you know the greatness of His plan—your part in it?
Do you know the greatness of His power—that is in you?
Do you know the greatness of His person—that is above all?
That is Paul's prayer for the church!
That is every believer's need!

ILL: A dear Christian lady lived near a seminary. The students all called her "grandma." She was a wonderful woman but could neither read nor write. A first-year student (those are the ones who have the answer to everything) told of a visit with "grandma." He intended to explain his vast knowledge of John 14 and make it simple so grandma could understand. She listened a while, then said, "Young man, have you ever noticed this in that chapter?" And then she went on to share marvelous, deep truths from the Scripture which the student had never read in books nor heard from professors. The young man (J. Vernon McGee) confessed he could not understand how she could have such deep insight into the Word when she could not even read or write. She knew things far beyond what he had learned in school. How did she know? The eyes of her heart had been opened by the Spirit of God.

❦ Chapter 2 ❧

FORMATION: GOD'S CHURCH-BUILDING PROGRAM

Ephesians 2:1-22

INTRO: This chapter presents the formation of the church in two strong considerations: materials and workmanship.

Part 1: THE MATERIALS (2:1–10)

I. THE PIT OF HUMAN DEPRAVITY (2:1–3)

    A. From Earth's Graveyard of Spiritual Death (v. 1)

    B. Along Life's Pathway of Human Rebellion (vv. 2–3)

II. THE SCENE OF DIVINE ACTIVITY (2:4–10)

    A. The True Origin of Our Salvation (v. 4)

    B. The Powerful Experience of Our Salvation (vv. 5–6)

    C. The Glorious Purpose of Our Salvation (vv. 7, 10)

III. GOD'S MASTERPIECE OF WORKMANSHIP (2:8–10)

    A. A Real Christian is the Product of Divine Workmanship (vv. 8–9)

    B. A Real Christian is the Creation of Spiritual Birth (v. 10a)

    C. A Real Christian is the Example of Eternal Design (v. 10b)

Part 2: THE WORKMANSHIP (2:11–22)

IV. THE MAKING OF THE CHURCH (2:11–13)

    A. A Reminder of Past Alienation (vv. 11–12)

    B. A Reassurance of Present Reconciliation (v. 13)

V. THE BROKEN WALL (2:14–18)

    A. There is the Crisis of Hostility! Hostility of Sin! (vv. 14–15)

    B. There is the Christ of Peace! Peace of God! (vv. 14, 15, 17)

VI. THE NEW HUMANITY (2:19–22)

    A. One New Nation Where God is Sovereign (v. 19a)

    B. One New Family of Which God is Head (v. 19b)

    C. One New Temple in Which God Dwells (vv. 20–22)

        1) The Foundation Stone (v. 20a)

        2) The Cornerstone (v. 20b)

        3) The Living Stones (v. 22)

Part 1: THE MATERIALS (2:1–10)

I. THE PIT OF HUMAN DEPRAVITY

"And you hath he quickened, who were
dead in trespasses and sins." (2:1)

Ephesians 2:1–3

INTRO: We have seen salvation from God's point of view. How that God has blessed us, chosen us, adopted us, made us accepted, redeemed us, forgiven us, called us, changed us by His Spirit. He has given us the Spirit of wisdom and revelation in the knowledge of Him so we may know His hope, His inheritance, and His power to upward who believe.

Now we are shown salvation from the perspective of the individual Christian. What we were before salvation. What Christ did for us in salvation. What we are to become because of the work of salvation in our lives.

This chapter begins with "And you"; the focus of that changes from God and the planning of the church to the individual believer and the building of the church.

The church in the world is "in the forming" like a house is "in the building." The church is a divine institution:

>God is the Designer—He designs its purpose.

>God is the Architect—He specifies its materials.

>God is the Builder—He fits the materials to specification.

>Christ is the Foundation—And no other can be laid.

>Christ is the Owner—He holds the title of ownership.

>God is the Occupant—"habitation of God through the Spirit."

See Matt. 16:18: "I [personally] will [positively] build [progressively] my church [privately]."

Note: Not "you will build my church," nor "I will build your church," but "I will build my church."

The church is a spiritual structure of which Christ is both the Head-Designer and Master-Builder. The material and workmanship are His.

This passage describes the material from which the church is built. God did not select angels nor heavenly beings of any kind. He came to earth and to fallen man, to the unrighteous Gentiles and the self-righteous Jews. He did not go to King's palaces, aristocratic section, or suburbia, but to skid row, to the pit of human depravity.

There He found material to build His church from two primary sources:

A. From Earth's Graveyard of Spiritual Death (v. 1)

1. The Real Problem With The Human Race! "You were dead."
2. Throughout the whole history of humanity, there have been three basic views of human nature.

    a) Man is doing morally quite well and getting better. People are basically okay and all is well. They will admit that human nature is not as healthy as it may perhaps one day be. Man is only slightly flawed and is growing better by passing time.
    b) Man is still alive and there is some hope. Man is not well, he is sick. But the situation is not hopeless. People are at least alive. As long as there is life there is hope of improvement.
    c) Man is morally and spiritually dead in trespasses and sins. That is the Biblical view which Paul articulates strongly here. "You were dead." What does he mean? Man is dead—dead so far as his relationship to God is concerned. He is spiritually dead. Not "almost dead," not desperately ill, but actually dead. There is no life there. Look at the exact opposite—life. The Bible always describes/defines life in terms of our relationship to God. (See John 17:3; 1 John 5:11–12.)

1) Then, life is to know God. To be in relationship to God. To share the life of God. To be blessed of God. To have God's Son as our Savior. That alone is life.

2) Those living in sin are dead. Living dead. Walking zombies. They are ignorant of God. They do not know God. Existing physically but not living spiritually.

3. Sin is a killer. Sin kills.

   a) Sin kills innocence! No one is ever the same after he has sinned. ILL: Psychologists say a person never forgets anything. It may not be in our conscious memory. But everything we ever did, saw, or heard is buried somewhere in our subconscious memory. The result is sin leaves a permanent effect on a person. When innocence is lost, it can never be recovered and it is replaced by guilt. Guilt remains until the conscience is seared or the sin is forgiven.

   b) Sin kills ideals: any standard of good or excellence. In so many lives there is a kind of tragic process.

      1) At first a man regards some wrong thing with horror.

      2) The second stage is when he is tempted to do the wrong thing, but even if he yields, he is unhappy and very conscious that it is wrong.

      3) The final stage of compromise is when he repeats the thing so often that he can do it w/o any compunction or scruples. Each sin makes the next sin easier. Sin kills the scruples that make life worth living.

   c) Sin kills the will! At first a person engages in some sinful pleasure because he wants to do so. At last he does it because he cannot help doing so. Once a thing becomes a habit, it's not far from being a necessity. When some forbidden practice, habit, indulgence masters a person, he becomes its slave. Sin kills the will; the thing so grips him that he cannot break free.

4. The Tragic Issues of Human Life! (Dead of what?)

    a) "Sin" Greek: HAMARTIA, a shooting word. LIT. "a miss." A man shoots his arrow at the target; the arrow misses; that is HAMARTIA. Sin is the failure to hit the target of life. Common wrong ideas of sin. It is easy to call a robber, murderer, drunkard, gangster a sinner. But since most people are respectable citizens, we think sin has little to do with us. The plain fact is that sin is the failure to be what we could/ought to be, missing the real purpose of life—as a husband, father, son, employee, or citizen. It is failure—missing life's real purpose.

    b) "Trespasses" Gr: PARAPTOMA, LIT. "to slip or fall." It is used of a man losing the way and trying from the right road. Trespass is taking the wrong road when we could take the right road. It is a failure to reach the goal we should have reached. The central idea of sin is failure: to hit the target, to take the right road, failure to make life what it is capable of becoming.

B. Along Life's Pathway of Human Rebellion (vv. 2–3)

This passage has the sound of rebellion vs. God in it. The word "wherein" goes back to "trespasses and sins." This took place in the "time past" of our lives. "Walked" Gr: "to live, to regulate one's life, to conduct oneself, order one's behavior." Paul here reveals the triad of evil which controls the sinful, rebellious lifestyle:

1. The World, the spirit of evil! (v. 1:2a)

    A) LIT: "the spirit of the age." According to secularism. The way of the world. The principle of the world.

    b) The "world" does not refer to the physical universe. It means the cosmos, society, civilization, life-pattern, a lifestyle of the world today. The way this present world lives. The world's standards/values. Biblically the world is the outlook, the mentality, and the organization of life apart from God. View of life w/o God. God is shut out. Man control w/o God.

2. The Devil, the Prince of Evil! (v. 2b)

   a) The Devil is so subtle that he dominates man and persuades him at the same time that he is not being dominated.

   b) The Devil is called "the god of this world." Sinful men by nature are under the dominion of Satan. He stood up and rebelled against God because he wanted to be God. He hates God. His one object is to mar God's creation and ruin God's world.

   c) He has his forces, his powers. He is "the prince." Of what? The powers of the air (unseen powers; see 6:12).

   d) This "spirit" worketh ("energizes") those who are willfully disobedient to God.

3. The Flesh, the Nature of Evil! (v. 3)

   a) Sinful man is enslaved by his own sinful cravings which he is always at work to gratify. "Flesh" does not refer to our skin. But to our fallen sinful nature, including both fleshly desires and wicked thoughts.

   b) Some fleshly sins are obvious: gluttony, laziness, lust, greed.

   c) Some are of the inner-intellect sort: pride, sinful ambition, hostility to truth, malice, and envy. These fleshly cravings make the unbeliever the object of the wrath of God.

CONCL: This is where God found all of us. In the pit of human depravity. In the graveyard of moral death. Along the pathway of spiritual rebellion. (See 1 Cor. 6:9–11; Psalm 40:2.)

ILL: Jesus walked the highway of time, and along the pathway of spiritual rebellion, the road to destruction, He picked up the pieces of discarded human wreckage and remade them to fit into His church.

ON THE ROAD TO JERICHO, a dying man, robbed and stripped. "I can use him to build My church." He carefully picked him up, remade him to fit into the church.

ON THE ROAD TO JERUSALEM, a crying man, blind and begging. "I can use him to build My church." He compassionately picked him up, remade him to fit into His church.

ON THE ROAD TO DAMASCUS, a defying man, hating and hurting. "I can use him to build My church." Knocked him down, struck him blind, made him over, raised him up, sent him out to be a church-builder.

ON THE ROAD TO NOWHERE, He found a nobody like you and me. "I can use them to build My church." Carefully picked up all the pieces, made us over to fit into His church.

ON THE ROAD TO HELL AND DESTRUCTION, He finds heaps of human wreckage, goes where they are, picks up the pieces out of the horrible pit, remakes them to fit into His church. (See vv. 1–3 AMP.)

II. THE SCENE OF DIVINE ACTIVITY

(Our Salvation)

"But God, who is rich in mercy, for his great love wherewith he loved us." (2:4)

Ephesians 2:4–10

INTRO: In the first verses of this chapter, we are given a look into the pit of human depravity. It begins with "And you" and follows with a graphic description of the sinner's condition. There in the graveyard of spiritual death men are dead in trespasses and sins. They have totally missed the mark in life. They have missed the right way and wandered down the wrong road in life. They are caught up in secularism, the spirit of this evil world. Their life is dominated by the prince of evil himself. Their behavior is ordered by the lustful cravings of their Adamic nature. They are indeed the objects of God's divine wrath.

This passage begins with "But God"! It resumes the thought of (v. 1) God's life-giving power. These words obviously suggest a connection with something that has gone on before.

A connection between a rebellious man and a loving God.

A contrast between a sinful man and a merciful

God. In a sense they contain the whole gospel.

There follows what God has done for fallen man. God's intervention in a sinful world.

Here the pit of human depravity becomes the scene of divine activity. These verses describe God's redemptive activity on behalf of depraved humanity.

A. The True Origin of our Salvation! (v. 4)

Three words are employed here showing the true origin of our salvation. Answer to, why did God do all this for us? The conjunction "but" contrasts the depths of depravity to which man had sunk to the ample resources of God's divine grace.

1. We Are Saved Because of God's Rich Mercy!

   a) Man is spiritually dead. A complete failure. He is incapable of saving himself. God comes on this scene of death with His mercy. God's justice would have destroyed us. Only divine mercy could save us. (See Rom. 10:12; 11:32.)

   b) God does not come too late with too little. He has a surplus, infinite, rich mercy. For poor sinners, He has rich mercy. That means enough and then some.

   c) ILL: A poor woman from the slums of London was invited to go with a group for an all-expense-paid holiday to the ocean. She had never been to the coast, and when she saw the ocean for the first time she burst into tears. Those around her thought it strange that she should cry when such a lovely holiday had been given her. They asked, "Why in the world are you crying?" Pointing to the ocean, "This is the only thing I have ever seen that there is enough of."

2. We Are Saved Because of God's Great Love! "But God . . . for His great love wherewith he loved us."

   a) A combination of the same word is used only when the idea of the verb is to be intensified. Difference between His mercy and His love. Love is the fountain of mercy. Mercy is the manifestation of His great love. Love is the root. Mercy is the fruit.

   b) Love is more than an attribute of God. It is the very nature of God, the essence of God. No wonder NT says, "God is love."

   c) God loved us when we were dead. His love does not depend on what we are, but on Who He is. So God descends into the pit of human depravity with only two tools: Hammer of love; Chisel of mercy.

d) ILL: See John 3:16, which says loud and clear, God loves you and has given Heaven's best for your welfare.

3. We Are Saved Because of God's Free Grace! (v. 5b)

a) This seems to be the ultimate word that clarifies forever the true origin of our salvation. It is repeated in an almost identical sentence in the latter half of this same paragraph (v. 5): "by grace ye are saved." (See vv. 8–9.)

b) Saved, not of yourselves. Not of works. It is the free, sovereign favor of our Lord. Salvation is given by grace. It is appropriated by faith-trust in Christ. Oh the miracle, the mystery, the marvel of it. The great God of Heaven and earth loves us cross-grained, rough-edged, self-centered, ill-tempered bundle of neuroses, and gives us His gift of eternal life.

c) Salvation is wholly of God, plus nothing at all.

B. The Powerful Experience of Our Salvation! (vv. 5–6)

1. The Holy Spirit coined three new Greek words here (vv. 5–6), unknown to the then-used language, to express the powerful experience of salvation. They communicate the radical change in the believer brought about by the unmerited kindness of God. Dead now alive.

a) Slaves now set free. We were objects of God's wrath; now we have experienced God's love. How can it be described, expressed?

b) The most powerful thing that God ever did—the Resurrection and Ascension of Christ!

c) Nothing like this had been known in the history of the world. No surprise that adequate words did not exist to describe it. So the Holy Spirit coined three new words through Paul.

d) He took a small prefix Gr: SYN, "together with," and combined it with three words used elsewhere to describe the most powerful thing that God ever did. The resurrection and ascension of Jesus: "Made alive—raised up—seated down."

2. In salvation we are Made Alive Together with Christ!

   a) New Gr. word: SYZOPOIEO, "to make alive together with." We were dead, now alive. It is a spiritual quickening. (See Col. 2:13; John 5:21; John 6:63.)

   b) It is an experiential term. It happened at conversion when we were born again. The Holy Spirit breathed spiritual life into us. We are alive from the dead like the prodigal. New life has been imparted and implanted. Now we have a new disposition, a new nature, a new man-creature.

3. In salvation we are Raised Up Together with Christ!

   a) New Gr. word: SYNEGEIRO, "to raise up together with."

   b) Refers to a spiritual resurrection. Not human resuscitation. But divine resurrection from death of sin.

   c) After God gives us life, He sets us on our feet. God raises fallen man up and puts him on his feet. (See Ps. 40:2; Rom. 6:4.)

   d) ILL: When God made Adam, He breathed into his nostrils the breath of life. God did not leave him lying there, a living, breathing creature, but He set him on his feet to walk and live upon earth among the world.

4. In salvation, we are Seated Together with Christ!

   a) New Gr. word: SYNKATHIZO, "to sit down together with."

   b) Refers to our ascension into a heavenly realm. When salvation is experienced, we are not taken up into heaven immediately. But indeed we are raised up, taken up into a heavenly realm. We are no longer creatures of this world only.

   c) Bound by our senses. We are now part of a heavenly kingdom. We have a new standard of values with spiritual priorities. We are part of the kingdom of God right here on earth. (See Col. 3:1–2.)

C. **The Glorious Purpose of Our Salvation! (vv. 7, 10)**

Twofold purpose shown here: That the *power* and *glory* of grace may be manifested by the saints. The phrase "in the ages to come" LIT: "in the ages that are coming one upon another." It refers to both the ages of human history and the ages of eternity.

1. That the Power of Grace may be Manifested in the Ages of Time by the Saints! (v. 10)

    a) The saints are the workmanship of God. They are the creation of grace—"unto good works." They are not saved "BY" good works, but "UNTO" good works. (See Matt. 5:16.)

    b) We are a living demonstration of what God's grace can do. God is merciful-loving-gracious, and we are the proof.

    c) Paul, "I am what I am by the grace of God." We are not self-made but made by grace.

2. That the Glory of Grace may be Displayed in the Ages of Eternity by the Saints! (v. 7)

    a) The saints are the trophies of grace. ILL: Someday we will be on display, on exhibit. In eternity the angels of heaven will point to a redeemed saint and say, "See that Christian there. He was lost and not worth saving, but he is here in Heaven today. It is only through the grace and kindness of God that he was saved and brought here."

    b) In the eternal ages we shall show forth "the exceeding riches of His grace in his kindness toward us." We will display and exhibit what God's grace has accomplished. ILL: 3:10 (emphasis mine): "To the intent that now unto the principalities and powers in heavenly places might be known by the church the *manifold* wisdom of God."

        1) "Manifold" Gr: multiformed. It describes a floral display consisting of variegated flowers and colors of rare beauty.

        2) Then all heaven will recognize the wisest thing God ever did is to bring all men together into one body, the church.

CONCL: This old sin-cursed earth, the pit of human depravity, is now the scene of divine activity. The God of mercy, love, and grace is at work. Through His Spirit, His Word, and His people. God is at work! Quickening the spiritually dead. Raising fallen man to his feet again. Seating them in the kingdom of heaven right here on this earth. Those saved by grace are still saved by resurrection power. They are the trophies of His grace. They are the workmanship of God. They are the creation of grace unto good works.

Note the contrast: "And you"—"But God."

And you were dead, But God gives life.

And you were rebellious, But God is merciful.

And you were down in sin, But God raises to newness of life.

And you were on the wrong road, But God brings you back.

"And you"?

What about you?

III. GOD'S MASTERPIECE OF WORKMANSHIP

"For we are his workmanship, created in Christ
Jesus unto good works, which God hath before
ordained that we should walk in them." (2:10)

Ephesians 2:8–10

INTRO: Occasionally one observes something of rare quality and skilled workmanship. You admire the beauty of its excellence. Usually the first thing you want to know is the manufacturer. You look for the label. Who is the maker, the creator of this exceptional product?

Whenever you are privileged to encounter a real-true-NT Christian, you are struck with the wonder, the marvel, the character of such a person. And be well assured if you could find a label, it reads, "Made By God's Grace." Christian confession, "By the grace of God, I am what I am."

In fact, all creation carries the stamp of God's workmanship. Anything God makes is quality. It is good.

ILL: At the first creation when "God created the heavens and the earth." 1st Day, light from nothing, "it was good"; 2nd Day, the firmament, atmospheric heavens, "it was good"; 3rd Day, land and vegetation, "it was good"; 4th Day, sun, moon, stars, "it was good"; 5th Day, animal life, "it was good"; 6th Day, "Man in His own image and likeness." (See Gen. 1:31.)

But just wait till you see His new creation. Fallen, broken man—remade by God's grace; reborn by God's Spirit. That is the masterpiece of His workmanship.

God did a glorious work in creation, but the work of salvation is His masterpiece. God does a great work in raising the dead—healing the sick, wonders, miracles, but the work of salvation is His masterpiece.

Oh the wonder of the work of salvation. It is from sin and degradation (vv. 1–3), by love—God's great love (v. 4), into life—spiritual life (v. 5), with purpose to display God's kindnesses (vv. 6–7), through faith in

Christ (vv. 8–9), and unto good works, the evidence of faith (v. 10). That is the masterpiece of His workmanship.

This passage is a glorious description of what it means to be a real NT Christian. We have already seen God's eternal plan, His design for man. Now these verses show us how God forms and makes the Christian to bring His design to reality.

A. A Real Christian is the Product of Divine Workmanship! (vv. 8–9)

There are three times when God works totally alone, all by Himself: Creation, Redemption, and Salvation. These two verses show us how in salvation, God works alone.

1. Salvation comes from the source of God's grace, "by grace are ye saved."

    a) That is the fountainhead, the springs, the source of salvation. Grace is the free, undeserved favor of God. From it we get our words "gratis" and "gratuity."
    b) It occurs in a business phrase "three days of grace," for payment of a bill. Grace is a divine manifestation to which man is not entitled, did not deserve it, earn it, nor desire it.

2. Salvation is appropriated by personal faith which is God-given, "through-faith." Faith is the channel through which grace flows to us individually.
3. Salvation is from no selfish source, "not of yourselves." No man can save himself by any means, nor pick himself up by his own bootstraps.
4. Salvation is from no human source; "it is the gift of God." Nothing man can do can save a soul.
5. Salvation is from no source of works, "not of works." Cannot be earned. Not on a merit scale. Good works are the object of salvation, not the source of salvation.
6. Salvation allows no human boasting, "lest any man should boast." Our only claim is "by grace through faith."
7. Salvation is God's work alone, "for we are his workmanship."

a) V. 10 is a summary of vv. 8–9. Salvation is not produced nor earned by man. It is the free gift of God without strings attached. That eliminates human boasting. Grace glorifies God.

b) Works glorify man. The "new man" is not self-made; not man-made; but he is God–made.

c) We cannot boast, for we are His workmanship. The handiwork of God, God's new creation.

B. A Real Christian is the Creation of Spiritual Birth! (v. 10a)

"For we are his workmanship, created in Christ Jesus unto good works." "Created in Christ Jesus" is a further definition of "his workmanship." "Workmanship" Gr: POIEMA, "something that is made from nothing." Like a literary poem.

1. We are part of God's new creation. The Christian is a new creation. A new creature by new birth. (See 2 Cor. 5:17; Col. 3:10; Gal. 6:15.)

2. We are part of a complete restoration. Salvation is not the repair of the ravages and ruptures of fallen man, but a new creation, a new man.

a) ILL: Henry Moorehouse, a social worker in the worst slum district of the city of London in the last century, tells a story that illustrates perfectly the grace of God in Salvation. He saw a little girl come out of a store carrying a pitcher of milk. As she approached her house, she tripped, fell, and broke the pitcher. Milk spilled everywhere. She began to cry bitterly. Moorehouse went to her, helped her to her feet, "Don't cry, child; everything's all right." But there was no stopping the tears. "My mommy'll punish me." He consoled, "No, dear, your mother won't spank you. I'll see to that. Look, the pitcher isn't broken in many pieces." As he stooped down beside her, picked up the pieces, and began putting the pitcher back together, the girl stopped crying. Hope arose. She had seen mother repair pitchers. Maybe this man can repair the damage. She watched as the man put several pieces together, then fumbled and knocked it apart again.

She began crying again. "Don't cry, dear, I promise you your mother won't punish you." Once more he attempted the task of restoration. Get it all together except the handle and then break it apart again. This time there was no stopping the tears. Finally the gentleman picked her up in his arms, carried her to a shop down the street and bought a new pitcher, carried her to the milk store, and filled it up. He asked her where she lived and carried her to her house, sat her down on her steps, placed the full pitcher of milk in her hands, and opened the door for her. "Now, do you think your mother will punish you?" Through a bright smile, "Oh, no, sir, because it's a lot better pitcher than we had before."

b) When Adam fell, he broke the image of God beyond repair. A new man had to be bought by Christ at Calvary.

C. A Real Christian is the Example of Eternal Design!

"Unto good works, which God hath before ordained that we should walk in them" (v. 10b). Before the foundation of the world, it was ordained that whoever is saved by grace should walk in good works. The "works" here have two special characteristics:

1. They are "GOOD" works!

   a) The Bible speaks of the works of the law, the works of the flesh, the works of darkness, and dead works. These are the pursuits of the old life of sin.

   b) But for the Christian (see Matt. 5:16), good works are no mystery. Just the inevitable law of love.

   c) ILL: If some great person loves us, we know it is not deserved. But we also know with deep conviction that we must spend the rest of our life trying to be worthy of it.

      1) This is our relationship with God regarding good works.

      2) God loves us and we know we do not deserve it. But God's favor-love gives us a sense of obligation to try throughout our life to be worthy of it.

2. They are PREPARED works! "God hath before ordained that we should walk in them."

   a) "Ordained" means to prepare before, make ready beforehand.
   b) These are the pre-arranged, pre-designed moral standards of the new creation. Thereby good works and good deeds are the natural and necessary outcome of salvation by faith.

      1) "Walk in them" Gr: "to regulate one's life, to conduct one's life to order one's behavior."
      2) God's purpose was to make good works the element of our life—the domain in which our actions should move.
      3) We know what God wants us to do! God prepared long beforehand the lifestyle He wants us to live. Sent us His Son. Gave us His Word. So we seek to live the kind of life which will be pleasing to God.
      4) Good works are a necessary part of the faith by which we are saved because faith without works is dead. (See James 2:17.)
      5) A disposition inclined to good works is a necessary part of God's new creation. (See Luke 6:45.)
      6) Good works are a testimony of faith to men which glorify God.
      7) Good works are the criteria by which believers will be judged on the great day of the Lord.

CONCL: This is God's pre-planned design for our lives. (See Rom. 8:29.)

That is why Paul could say to the Philippians (1:6): "he which hath begun a good work in you will perform it until the day of Jesus Christ."

ILL: I read the story of a rowdy, disruptive young boy in a Sunday school class who continually frustrated the teacher. One morning the teacher asked him, "Why do you act like that? Don't you know Who made you?" To which the boy replied, "God did, but He ain't through with me yet."

God's great work in us will not cease until that great day, "when he shall appear, we shall be like him, for we shall see him as he is" (1 John 3:2 KJ21).

God can restore—renew a broken heart, broken man, shattered life, if you give Him all the pieces.

ILL: Broken pieces! I read of a famous old-world cathedral which contained a beautiful stained-glass window. It was a very popular tourist attraction. Beautiful and lovely. A great storm swept the country that shattered the window into a thousand tiny fragments. The pieces were gathered up and stored away in a box in the basement.

One day a stranger came to see the famous window. Upon finding out it had been destroyed, he asked whether he might have the pieces.

After many weeks he invited the owners of the cathedral to visit his studio. When they arrived, he took them into a room before a canvas curtain.

At the touch of his hand on a cord, the curtain fell, and there before their astonished eyes was the most beautiful colored stained-glass window they had ever seen. They admired its rich tints, marvelous workmanship, and cunning design.

"This I have wrought from the fragments of your broken window. It is ready to take its place again in the cathedral."

In just the same way God takes the broken pieces of our lives and refashions them into a unique design. (See v. 10; vv. 8–10 AMP.)

Part 2: THE WORKMANSHIP (2:11–22)

IV. THE MAKING OF THE CHURCH

"For we are his workmanship, created in Christ Jesus unto good works, which God hath before ordained that we should walk in them." (2:10)

Ephesians 2:11–13

INTRO: This is a point of transition in this chapter.

There is a definite break here and a new idea, a new thought is taken up. The *first part* of this chapter (vv. 1–10) deals with the plan of salvation. Man has fallen into the pit of human depravity. That pit became the scene of divine activity. From nothing God formed a new creation whose life of good works conforms in likeness to Jesus Christ's.

The text is a transitional verse applying to what is before and what is to follow. The word "for" (v. 10) points backward. The word "wherefore" (v. 11) leads forward: From individual salvation to corporate building of the body of Christ.From the saving of the individual to the making of the church. Both the Christian and the Church are the handiwork of God, His workmanship.

The great object of this epistle is to expound God's grand purpose in this present age. God's ultimate purpose is given in summary (1:10): "That in the dispensation of the fullness of times he might gather together in one all things in Christ, both which are in heaven, and which are on earth; even in him."

Sin has brought alienation, division, polarization, separation.

Unity is God's divine purpose for His created order. Christ is the Divine Agent for consummation of God's eternal plan.

The church is the Dynamic Center for the consummation of the eternal plan of the ages. The existence of the church is the sign that the work of redemption, which will ultimately unite all things, has begun. What a vision for the church! The gathering together of all separated, divided, polarized humanity into one body. What power would be gained if the church could only recover that self-understanding!

Here Paul shows the Ephesus Gentiles and all Gentiles what a tremendous thing it was that they should ever have become a Christian, and members of the Christian church.

This passage reveals God's great workmanship in The Making of The Church. The Making of The Church is explained by heavy ideas.

A. A Reminder of Past Alienation! (vv. 11–12)

1. It is a Social Alienation Evidenced by Barriers! (v. 11)

   a) Sin alienates man from God, other men, and himself. It is a part of sinful nature to build barriers that shut other people out. Uniqueness and distinctiveness lead to building barriers of superiority which condemn all others.

   b) These social barriers in NT times are quite obvious:

      1) The barrier between slaves and freemen. Those who were free looked down on slaves as being inferior, just slightly above animals. Slaves looked upon freemen and their masters with contempt and resentment. One of the greatest problems in the NT church was getting Christian freemen and Christian slaves to accept and treat each other as spiritual equals.

      2) The barrier between men and women. Women in NT times were looked down on as inferior beings. Husbands often treated their wives no better than a slave. When a woman became a Christian, she was often divorced by her husband because she made such a radical decision without his consent.

      3) The barrier between Greeks and Barbarians. The Greeks were so proud of their culture and supposed

racial superiority, they considered everyone else to be barbarians. Paul refers to this belief in Rom. 1:14 and Col. 3:11. All the other Gentiles resented the high-brow, snooty attitude of the intellectual Greeks.

4) The barrier between Jew and Gentile. Jews felt themselves a special people, a chosen people, and thereby superior to all those Gentile nations. Circumcision was the mark of Jewry. Gentiles were looked down on and condemned as "The Uncircumcised" and dogs. They were outcasts, "Gentiles in the flesh, . . . called Uncircumcision."

2. It is a Spiritual Alienation Confirmed by Despair! (v. 12)

a) Before salvation Jews and Gentiles alike are "dead in transgressions and sins."

b) But Paul argues the condition of the Gentiles is even worse. One word best describes the Gentile, "without." On the outside with a barrier between:

1) Without Christ, "at that time ye were without Christ." No expectation of a Savior. They are pagan. No knowledge of Christ, no interest in Him, no life or blessing from Him. Any unsaved person is "outside Christ," and that means condemnation and damnation.

2) Without Citizenship, "being aliens from the commonwealth of Israel." Israel was a special nation. They were God's nation in a way that was not true of any other nation. The Gentiles were foreigners with no right to expect salvation as did the children of Israel.

3) Without Promise, "strangers from the covenants of promise." God's covenant of promise with Abraham was that He would bless the world through Israel. God made no covenant with any Gentile nation. Gentiles are "aliens and strangers," and the Jews never let them forget it. Strangers to the Messianic covenants of promise made with Israel.

4) Without Hope, "having no hope." It is said the most dreadful word in a language is "useless." Yet the most terrible word is "hopeless." No hope means despair. All

is lost. There is nothing. Gentiles had not even a glimmer of hope to get to God.

5) Without God, "and without God in the world." God is the source of every good thing, including hope. Without God none can have any real hope that things will ever be good or get better. Without God we are without everything despite appearances to the contrary.

c) What a dark description of the condition of the Lost: outcasts, Christless, homeless, friendless, hopeless, and Godless! A grim picture. It all adds up to despair.

B. A Reassurance of Present Reconciliation! (v. 13)

"But now in Christ Jesus ye who sometimes were far off are made nigh by the blood of Christ." V. 12 is the darkest verse in the Bible, and v. 13 is the brightest. One describes alienation, the other reconciliation. Reconcile means "to bring together again the changing of places, coming over from one side to the other." It is the changing of judicial status from estrangement to acceptance, from condemnation to justification.

1. That Change is Affirmed By Great Contrast! In v. 12, "ye were"; in v. 13, "but now." It is the contrast between THEN AND NOW; BEFORE AND AFTER; BC AND AD!

   a) Before YOU WERE "without Christ"; separate from Christ. "But Now" you are (v. 13) "in Christ Jesus . . . made nigh by the blood of Christ." "All things in Christ." (See 1:13 NIV.)

   b) Before YOU WERE "aliens from the commonwealth of Israel." Excluded from citizenship. "But Now." (See v. 19; Phil. 3:20.)

   c) Before YOU WERE "strangers [foreigners] from the covenants of promise." Foreigners to promise. "But Now." (See 3:16.)

   d) Before YOU WERE "having no hope"; hopeless in total despair. "But Now." (See 4:4.)

e) Before YOU WERE "without God in the world"; Godless in an atheistic world. "But Now" (see 3:16): you are reconciled. Also see 3:19–20: You are members.

2. That Change is Accomplished by The Gracious Cleansing!

   a) You were "afar off" But Now "made nigh." "Made nigh" means brought near. The Jewish priest said this of every Jewish proselyte.

   b) Brought near to God as result of Christ's atonement for sin.

   c) Brought near to each other to form a new unity, the church.

   d) The alienated, separated, divided were "made nigh by the blood Christ." All barriers are made of sin. The blood of Christ washes them away.

   e) ILL: One illustration of this barrier-breaking is the cleansing of the leper to which this probably refers. To the Jew, the leper was a walking parable of death and judgment. He was alienated from society. He walked with bowed head. He dressed in distinctive garments. He carried a long staff in his hand. He cried, "Unclean, unclean!" to prevent anyone from coming into contact with him. He was an island in the sea of humanity. His existence was indeed "afar off," barricaded from other men. He could not enter the court of Israel, nor the court of priests. If a leper was cured, he had to be examined by the priest outside the camp, "afar off." But when he was pronounced clean, the sin offering was made for him, and he was led by the priest to the tabernacle of the congregation. He was permitted to enter into the court of Israel and worship God. We were lepers, outside the camp, having no privilege to enter into the courts of God's people. God took away the leprosy of sin, cleansing us in His precious blood, and ushered us into the holiest of all, into the presence of God.

CONCL: This is a tremendous change. A radical change. But we must not take it for granted. A key word in this passage is "remember." We must remember, lest we forget. Forget the pit from whence we were dug. Forget the blessings to which we have come. We must not become insensitive. We must not despair of God's ability to save others.

ILL: John Newton of a past century was converted as a slave trader. God brought him from a position of utter wretchedness to a preacher of the gospel. Once a fellow minister was talking with him about the salvation of a very wicked man. And asked him if he did not despair of the salvation of such a hard, vile sinner. Newton replied, "I never did despair since God saved me." ("He can save anyone.")

That's what it means to remember.

Remember what we were.

Remember what we have become.

Remember and expect to see the same change in others.

"Remember" in a scriptural sense means more than just a keeping in mind, or mental recall.

It means a continued rehearsing and restructuring and involving oneself in the realities of some past event.

"Remember Pearl Harbor" and "Remember the Alamo" mean much more than just dates in history.

V. THE BROKEN WALL

*"For he is our peace, who hath made both one, and hath
broken down the middle wall of partition between us." (2:14)*

Ephesians 2:14–18

INTRO: The startling news of a significant historical event shocked the world recently. The Berlin Wall that divided East and West Germany for about half a century has been broken down. Access to both sides of the country is restored. The political enmity, hostility, and hatred of the fragmented German people have been abolished. Now the popular opinion is the reunification, reconciliation of East and West into one Germany again.

This section of Scripture deals with the reconciliation of divided humanity. God's ultimate purpose is the unity of all alienated humanity into one body, the church.

Before this purpose could be realized, God had to deal with the radical division.

The cause of the alienation is sin. This truth is explained step by step in vv. 1–13. It begins with the emphatic statement that sin produces death (vv. 1–10). He goes one step further to state how sin always leads to separation (vv. 11–13). In this passage (vv. 14–18), he arrives at the apex of the problem, that is, sin puts man at enmity. It builds hostility. It creates hatred.

So among men, there are walls and wars. Barriers and conflict. Hatred and hostility. Differences and divisions.

God's Kingdom could never exist in such a hostile environment. Therefore, God deals with the enmity.

ILL: Time and wars on earth: Only 8% of the time since the beginning of recorded history has the world been entirely at peace, according to stats.

I read somewhere that from 1500 BC to AD 850 there were 7,500 "eternal covenants" agreed upon among various nations with the hope of bringing peace. Yet no peace treaty has lasted longer than 2 years.

The only "eternal covenant" of peace that has lasted and will last is the one made by the eternal God, sealed by the blood of Jesus Christ. V. 13: "But now in Christ Jesus ye who sometimes were far off are made nigh by the blood of Christ." What follows in vv. 14–18 is an explanation of that act of reconciliation.

In this passage we are shown the existence of hostility and the experience of peace.

A. There is the Crisis of Hostility! Hostility of Sin! (vv. 14–15)

Great enmities existed, polarization, fragmentation, division, alienation, variance, conflict, hostility, cause for estrangement, irreconcilable differences. This condition is expressed here in some illustrative words.

1. "Enmity"—The State of Enmity! "Enmity" (v. 15) Gr: "hostility, hatred." Repeated twice here.

   a) Enmity between Jew/Gentile or man/man. The root cause of all enmity is the pride of man. Feeling of superiority. Spirit of exclusiveness.
   b) Enmity (v. 16) between man and God. In fact, the root of sin against God is the pride of man. Sin is essentially pride, self-autonomy. Satan's approach in garden, "Hath God said?" Who is this to tell you what to do? Stand on your own dignity. Demand your personal rights. It led to the fall and all its appalling consequences. Self-pride, self-interest, self-love, self-praise. Man sets himself up as god. It puts him at enmity against the God of Heaven.

2. "Wall"—The Wall of Partition!

   a) Walls are built to separate. Partition means to keep apart.
   b) ILL: It is a definite reference to the Jewish Temple. Inside the Temple walls were a series of courts. The innermost court

was the hallowed Holy of Holies into which the high priest only could go once a year. Then came the Court of Priests, where the priest alone could enter for service. Then came the Court of Israel, where men only could enter. Then came the Court of Women, for Jewish women only. Then finally, the outermost court, far back and away from the holiest, far away from even priests, separated from the men of Israel by a barrier of "lowly" women, was the Court of the Gentiles. Between the Women's Court and the Gentiles Court was a small 3-foot ornate wall. Stressing further the separation of Gentiles, a sign was posted here which read: "No foreigner is to enter the blockade and embankment around the sanctuary. Whoever is caught will have himself to blame for his death which follows."

3. "Afar Off"—The Position of Distance!

    a) ILL: As a leper was isolated from society, so by the leprosy of sin the sinner Gentile was forced by law to remain "afar off."

    b) ILL: It also refers to the Jewish Temple again. It consisted of a series of courts, each one a little higher than the one that went before, with the Holy of Holies being the innermost and the highest. The Court of Gentiles was the lowest level and the farthest away, "afar off" from the place where God's glory dwelt.

B. B. There is the Christ of Peace! Peace of God! (vv. 14, 15, 17)

The experience of peace is expressed powerfully here by three usages of the word "Peace." Each time that peace is related directly to Christ.

1. Christ Being Peace! "He is our peace" (v. 14).

    a) This phrase explains the previous verse, the way by which we were brought nigh. This One, by whose blood we have been made nigh, is our peace.

    b) The structure of grammar here gives us an emphatic (dlb) pronoun, "He"—"Himself." The emphasis is, Jesus Himself alone is our peace. There is no other source.

c) Christ is more than a Peacemaker, He is our peace. He is our peace in the fullest sense: The very substance of it. The living source of it. He arbitrates it in the beginning; He secures it to the end. ILL: Job's Daysman (see Job 9:32–33). A Daysman is a mediator who stands in a judicial capacity between parties at variance and brings peace. It was the Easter custom for the judge to lay his hand upon the heads of the two parties in disagreement and attempt reconciliation. So on the cross, Christ laid one hand on a Holy God and the other on sinful man and effected reconciliation, redemption by His blood.

d) The complex idea of peace in this verse is not only between Jew/Gentile, but between God and both. Made both one in Christ. Removed the wall between.

2. Christ Making Peace! "Abolished the enmity" (v. 15).

   a) "Enmity." The cause of the hostility was the legal principle of the Jewish Law. It made a definite distinction between Jews and other men. It made ridiculous demands that were impossible to keep.

   b) "Abolished" Gr: "to nullify." The Law cannot claim control over Jew/Gentile since in Christ believers are not under the Law but under grace. The righteousness of the Law, revealing God's Holiness, is still God's standard. It is fulfilled in us by the power of the Holy Spirit. (See Rom. 10:4.)

   c) "Making peace." Christ made peace by His work on the cross. The destroying of the enmity by the abolishing of the Law. The creating of a new man, the church, the body of Christ.

   d) "Make" Gr: "to create." The making of the church, the body of Christ, the new creation. The old was falling apart because of sin. But in the new creation there is unity because of righteousness. (See Gal. 3:28.)

3. Christ Proclaiming Peace! "Came and preached peace" (v. 17).

   a) "Preached" Gr: EVANGELIZO "to bring or announce good news."

b) It is almost always used in NT of proclaiming the gospel, the good news of salvation through Jesus Christ. It means not only to proclaim peace, but "he came and gospeled, evangelized peace."

c) The prophet (see Isa. 57:19):

1) This refers to Christ's peace mission when he came into the world. (See Luke 2:14.)

2) The disciples were to be "peacemakers" and proclaimers of peace.

3) To the 70. (See Luke 10:5.)

4) Among His last words. (See John 16:33.)

5) The NT church's ministry was characterized by "preaching peace through Jesus Christ." (See Acts 10:36 NKJV.)

6) The Holy Spirit is characterized by giving love, joy, and peace. (See Gal. 5:22.)

   a. The Kingdom of God is characterized by "righteousness and peace and joy in the Holy Ghost." (See Rom. 14:17 KJ21.)

   b. The peace with God. (See Rom. 5:1.)

   c. The peace of God. (See Phil. 4:7.)

CONCL: Sin had produced a world system of barriers. All mankind is divided. Separated from God, each other, and even themselves. To build His church, God had to deal with the division of humanity.

Paul used the illustration of the Temple layout to show what the blood of Christ had done. The barriers are made of sin. Therefore only the blood of Christ can wash them away (v. 13).

The dividing wall has been broken. The warning signs have been smashed. The enmity has been abolished. When Christ died on the cross, even the Temple veil was rent in two from top to bottom. The way is open for all to get to God. Those "far off" and those "near" have been reconciled, brought together in one body by the Cross. Now no one is excluded—all "have access by one Spirit to the Father."

The wall is broken. The barriers are down. The hostility is abolished. The signs are smashed. The enmity is removed. Access is opened.

You can get to the God of Heaven if you want to. At the cross the ground is level. We are all on equal footing. None is preferred (v. 18).

"Access" Gr: PROSAGO "to open a way of access." It was used of those who secure for one the privilege of an interview with a sovereign.

Access (entry) for all men: through Christ, by the Spirit, unto the Father. (See Heb. 4:15–16; 10:19–22.)

VI. THE NEW HUMANITY

"Now therefore ye are no more strangers and foreigners, but
fellowcitizens with the saints, and of the household of God." (2:19)

Ephesians 2:19–22

INTRO: All mankind on this planet, by nature and by culture, are hopelessly and helplessly divided among themselves.

In Bible times humanity was divided into two divisions: Jew and Gentile. In modern times the divisions are different, but very distinct. Today the divisions are political worlds. The Western World of democracy. The Eastern World of communism. The Third World countries.

God is making a new humanity. The new humanity is the church. It is a new society of mankind. It is a new man—a new creation in Christ Jesus (v. 15).

God did not intend to make Jews of Gentiles or Gentiles of Jews; Americans of Russians or Russians of Americans; but to make all men Christians together in one body, the church.

The New Humanity is made up of new creatures, who have experienced the new birth and who have entered into new life in Christ.

The old humanity is under the law dominated by sin. The new humanity is under grace controlled by righteousness. The old humanity is in the flesh. The new humanity is in the Spirit. The old in sin. The new in Christ.

"Now therefore" (v. 19) refers to the former passage where "the enmity" is abolished, "the wall" broken down, "the afar off" brought nigh, and the "peace" established in Christ.

Now therefore three things have happened: (1) We are "no more strangers." (2) We are no more foreigners. (3) We are now a new humanity joined together by Christ in the church.

The new humanity is presented here by three very expressive images: a kingdom, a family, and a temple.

A. One New Nation Where God is Sovereign! (v. 19a)

This is a rich field of imagery. The church, the new humanity, as the Kingdom of God. A city-state, a country, a nation.

1. The Kingdoms of Men!

    a) Of all the kingdoms of men, the Roman Empire was one of the greatest. The Kingdom of Rome was at the height of its territorial expansion and glory. This was in Paul's thoughts as he pictured the new humanity in which all men become "fellowcitizens with the saints." Rome dominated the entire known world.

    b) Roman armies kept peace and dispensed justice. Roman roads linked together the far reaches of the vast Empire. Rome had stood for hundreds of years and was thought to be invincible and eternal.

    c) However, Rome was not one united kingdom. It was a political power imposed on many hostile factions: rich-poor; free-slave; man-woman; Jew-Gentile.

    d) Paul saw in its place The New Humanity, united together by God Himself. The citizens of God's Kingdom are bound by a common ruler, live under common law, and share common rights/privileges.

    e) We are naturally born citizens of the Kingdom with birth certificates. Not foreigners living in a land on a passport. (See John 3:3.)

2. The Kingdom of God!

    a) God's Kingdom transcends all temporal concepts of its past, present, and future. Essentially, the Kingdom of God is where God rules.

    b) To God's past kingdom in the chosen nation of Israel. (See Matt. 21:43.)

    c) To God's people of the present, the apostle says, "Chosen generation." (See 1 Pet. 2:9-10.)

    d) Kingdom of God is in you. (See Luke 17:21; Rom. 14:17; 1 Cor. 4:20.)

e) The future new Jerusalem is called the Holy City. (See Matt. 25:34; Phil. 3:20–21.)

B. One New Family of Which God is Head! (v. 19b)

"Now therefore ye are no more strangers . . . but of the household of God." The second image of this new humanity, the church, is the family.

1. We Are Family Members!

   a) This is more than a household association. It means being born again into the Family of God with a relationship. (See John 3:7.)

   b) See John 1:12; Rom. 8:15–17; 1 Pet. 1:23 (NIV); 1 John 3:1.

   c) As children we bear a genetic likeness. There is a similarity, a continuity of nature. The life of the child is not the same life as the life of the parents. But it comes from them and is like theirs. It is called a genetic relationship in which parental characteristics are passed on to children. This is why there must be holiness in the church. God is holy. So God's children exemplify the characteristics of holiness. If not, then not children.

2. We Have Household Privileges!

   a) God's love binds us to the Father in holy sonship. He is our Father. It binds us to one another in holy brotherhood. We are a family. The experience that made us sons of God, at the same time made us brothers to one another. When we are born again, we become "sons" and "brothers" at the same time.

   b) It brings us the supportive network of our spiritual brothers and sisters.

   c) It gives us a share in the fellowship/discipline of the family.

   d) It gives us a right to a place in God's plan for His people.

   e) It gives us access to the Father, which means we can approach Him boldly in prayer.

C. One New Temple in Which God Dwells! (vv. 20–22)

Paul deals more extensively with the Temple image of the church. He speaks of the New Humanity, the church (vv. 20–22). This powerful temple picture of the church contains three very important aspects.

1. The Foundation Stone (v. 20a)

    a) The most important part of any structure. Its strength and durability depend on it. It must be right.

    b) The new humanity is built on the foundation laid by the apostles and prophets, which is Jesus Christ. By their teaching/work, they laid the foundation. (See 1 Cor. 3:11; Matt. 16:18.)

2. The Cornerstone (v. 20b)

    a) This passage calls Jesus both the Foundation and Cornerstone!

    b) ILL: A cornerstone was important for two reasons:

        1) It was part of the foundation.

        2) It was laid at the angle of the building and became the standard, the reference point from which came all the walls and arches throughout the building. (See Isa. 28:16.)

    c) ILL: The Psalmist wrote of a stone which the builders of Solomon's Temple rejected but which was later found and used (118:22).

    d) Jesus applied this Psalm to Himself. (See Matt. 21:42.)

    e) Now Peter tied these texts into one illustration. (See 1 Pet. 2:6–8.)

3. The Living Stones (v. 22)

    a) This passage does not specifically mention "living stones," but the same idea uses different words. (See v. 22 NIV.)

    b) God is at work through His Spirit and anointed workmen.

c) Believers are being joined to Christ the Cornerstone, and fitly framed together as the church continues to be built into a Holy Temple in the Lord. (See 1 Pet. 2:5 NIV.)

CONCL: So the church is a sacred building into which every member is intricately fitted. A Holy Temple. A Sacred Shrine. A Divine Sanctuary.

A permanent habitation of God by the Holy Spirit. Christ is the Foundation on which the grand spiritual Temple is built. He is the Cornerstone which shapes the whole building.

In Him the building is growing. Every soul saved is evidence that the work is going on. Sometimes it may seem slow, hard work, but yet the structure is rising, floor by floor. Ultimately that Temple will reflect without flaw its Indweller's Glory.

Built on the Son, by the Spirit, for the Father, this spiritual house is constructed of living stones.

Ah, the history of these stones. How rough, how hard, how unhewn. But they all pass through the hand of the Builder—each stone, one by one.

After hewing, chipping, squaring, shaping, and polishing, each stone fits perfectly into place.

In the OT, God is for us!

In Christ's Coming, God is with us!

In Spirit's Coming, God is in us! (See 2 Cor. 6:19; 3:16–17.)

❄ Chapter 3 ❄

EDIFICATION: GOD'S CHURCH GROWING AND DEVELOPING

Ephesians 3:1–21

INTRO: This chapter shows the growth and development of the church from two primary sources: the ministry of the Word and the ministry of prayer.

Part 1: THE MINISTRY OF THE WORD (3:1–12)

I.   WHEN A CHRISTIAN SUFFERS (3:1)

    A. There are No Complaints
    B. There is No Surrender to Fate
    C. There is a Purpose

II. THE MYSTERY OF THE CHURCH (3:2–6)

    A. Grace is Its Origin (v. 2)
    B. Known by Revelation (vv. 3–4)
    C. Hidden from Ages Past (v. 5)
    D. Explained in Detail (v. 6)

III. THE MAKING OF A MINISTER (3:7–8)

   A. The Minister of God (v. 7)
   B. The Message of the Gospel (v. 8)
   C. The Message of Christ

IV. MANIFESTING OF THE MYSTERY (3:9–12)

   A. Divine Purpose in Manifesting Wisdom (vv. 9–11)
   B. Human Privileges from Manifestation (v. 12)

Part 2: THE MINISTRY OF PRAYER (3:13–21)

V. THE PINNACLE OF PRAYER (3:14–19)

   A. The Strengthening of the Spirit (v. 16)
   B. The Indwelling of Christ (v. 17a)
   C. The Knowing of Love (vv. 17b–19a)
   D. The Filling of Fullness (v. 19b)

VI. THE TRIUMPH OF PRAISE (3:20–21)

   A. Declares the Sufficiency of God's Ability (v. 20a)
   B. Describes the Working of God's Power (v. 20b)
   C. Discloses the Eternality of God's Glory (v. 21)

Part 1: THE MINISTRY OF THE WORD (3:1–12)

I. WHEN A CHRISTIAN SUFFERS

"For this cause I Paul, the prisoner of Jesus
Christ for you Gentiles." (3:1)

Ephesians 3:1

INTRO: In ch. 2 it was the building of the church. Now ch. 3 deals with the edifying (sustaining, nourishing, strengthening) of the church. Edification denotes a sense of spiritual growth and character development in believers. It is spiritual growth resulting from patient labor in the Word and prayer. It is the finished work, detailed work of the Builder in perfecting of the edifice.

Here Paul strings together the two spiritual lifelines of the church. Reveals the church's double power source. Activates its spiritual generators. The Ministry of the Word (vv. 1–13) and the Ministry of prayer (vv. 14–21).

It begins with the phrase "For this cause." Refers to the idea in ch. 2 that God is gathering together all men into one body, the church. They were "dead in trespasses and sins" (2:1); "strangers," "aliens," with "no hope," "without God in the world" (2:12); now "made nigh" (2:13). All hostility removed, they are "fellowcitizens with the saints," members "of the household of God" (2:19), part of "a holy temple in the Lord" (2:21).

Having explained these truths, Paul says, "For this cause [because of this], I Paul the prisoner of Jesus Christ for you Gentiles." There he seems to stop. He obviously has more to say, but he pauses, he hesitates, he digresses, and he does not say it until he gets to v. 14, where we find the exact same phrase, "For this cause." (All this impels me to pray.) Then he goes on to say he is praying for them, and what he is praying for them. From vv. 2–13 is a long digression, a parenthetical statement on the ministry of preaching, after which he returns to the thought of prayer.

Why the interruption, parenthesis, digression? The answer is in v. 13: "Wherefore I desire that ye faint not at my tribulations for you, which is your glory."

When in v. 1 he introduces himself as "the prisoner of Jesus Christ," his immediate thoughts were, What effect will that news have on the saints? Will they be troubled that he is a prisoner in Rome? Will they worry about his health and future? Will his sufferings as a prisoner become a stumbling block to their faith? Why do Christians have to suffer?

So the Holy Spirit inspires Paul to show us the attitude of a real Christian when he suffers. How should a Christian respond in time of suffering? What are the great principles in facing the difficult problem of suffering?

The word is "when" a Christian suffers, not "if," for suffering is inevitable. There will in fact be suffering, sickness, sorrow, trouble, tribulation, trials, problems, pain, persecutions.

Why? How should we respond, When a Christian Suffers? The answer is in Paul's experience as a prisoner and his statement in v. 1.

A. There are No Complaints

1. We are great complainers.

   a) ILL: Like Israel. They complained vs. God, leadership, food, and the journey. As a result, they missed God's promise and purpose for them.

   b) ILL: Complain before we know. Like an old lady from the country had never visited the city much and just was not used to a hotel. The clerk assigned her to a room and told her the bellboy would take her bags and show her to her room. She followed the boy and then abruptly complained, "Why, I'd never think of taking this room. It's the smallest closet room I ever saw." The boy coolly answered, "Step in, madam, this isn't your room; this is the elevator."

   c) ILL: A man greeting a friend, "How's life?" Answer, "I would complain, but nobody really listens."

2. Paul's Sufferings Are Totally Ignored!

    a) He is in prison, but not one single word of complaint is uttered. Not even a suspicion of a grumble.

    b) He will not allow the questions to enter his mind and heart. Is this fair? I have served God for years, I have traveled, I have labored, I have suffered, I am old before my time, Why has this happened to me? Never a suspicion of that. Not a word. No complaint. No grumble.

    c) Paul's Secret Is Fairly Simple! He has learned a valuable spiritual lesson. He has gotten victory over complaints. (See Phil. 4:11–13.)

B. There is No Surrender to Fate

1. There seem to be two directions one can take in time of sufferings:

    a) You Can Surrender To Fate!

        1) Here the circumstances of one's life are controlled by some irresistible and foreordained forces. Date with destiny. Lot in life. My portion. My doom. That's just life. I can't do anything about it.

        2) Paul did not resign himself to trouble with a cold fatalism. Many do. But there is none of that here.

        3) He does not accept defeated attitudes: you have to take the bad with the good, or "every rose has a thorn" theory.

        4) The paganistic philosophy of life: I have enjoyed the good, now must endure the bad. There is no advice to pull yourself together, be a man, take courage, maintain a stiff upper lip. No such teachings of fate here. World's way.

    b) You Can Be a Survivor By Faith!

        1) Just because you suffer does not mean you have lost faith.

        2) Faith will do one of two things: Save you from the trouble, or take you through the difficulty victoriously.

Whichever, faith is at work. Sometimes it takes more faith to go through trouble than to be spared from it.

3) Whatever the circumstances in life, "the just shall live by faith" (Rom. 1:17).

C. There is a Purpose

1. Paul seems to be rejoicing in his trials and sufferings. There is a spirit of exultation here, a note of triumph, a sense of victory. (See v. 13.)

2. Right attitude and regal purpose. He wants them to be "more than conquerors" as he is (see Rom. 8:37). He is not merely putting up with the bad circumstances. He goes beyond that. He is exulting, rejoicing in sufferings. Triumphant. Jubilant.

3. The Doctrine Of Rejoicing In Christian Sufferings

   a) There is an NT doctrine of rejoicing in trouble. (See Phil. 1:12.)

   b) Don't waste pity and tears on me. Trouble has furthered the gospel. Thank God for it. (See John 16:33; 2 Tim. 1:7; 2:3, 12; 3:12; 1 Pet. 4:12–14; Jas. 1:2–3.)

4. The Practice of Rejoicing in Christian Sufferings!

   a) How do we Christians arrive at this position? Certainly not because of a mild, placid temperament. Paul was the opposite. Peace of mind, joy of spirit in times of trouble are not a matter of temperament. It is the product of spiritual reasoning employed. He asks questions, receives answers, and works out the solution.

   b) We must learn that secret. Instead of being overwhelmed by trouble, depressed by suffering, or defeated by it all, we must ask questions about the thing itself, not about God. Put the whole human situation in perspective. Relate it to the whole of Christian faith and life.

   c) Why am I a prisoner? What is the cause of this predicament? How has this happened? What are the reasons for it? In v. 1, the answers are given:

1) He is no ordinary prisoner!

   a. "Paul, the prisoner of Jesus Christ" (3:1). "The prisoner of the Lord" (4:1). "An ambassador in bonds" (6:20).

   b. This admission alone solves the problem. Not the prisoner of Rome, nor of Nero, nor of the Roman law. Not for some misdemeanor or crime. "Paul, the prisoner of Jesus Christ." What a staggering statement. In fact, everything of Paul is in relation to Christ, and because of Christ. Paul: the apostle, servant, minister, bond-slave of Christ. Now "prisoner" because he is "in Christ." Here, because of what happened to him at conversion. It is that event that has brought him to Rome and to prison.

2) He is suffering for Christ's sake! "For this cause."

   a. The cause of Christ. Remember his Damascus Road commission? (See Acts 9:16.)

   b. Not for Paul's sake but for Christ's sake. Not for any wrong he personally has committed, but because of his zeal for the name and glory of Christ. He is literally suffering as a Christian and for the sake of Christ. (See Phil. 1:29.)

   c. ILL: The NT believers regarded suffering for Christ the supreme honor of their lives.

   d. They thanked God they had been counted worthy to suffer for their Lord's sake. The final crown of glory was martyrdom.

3) He is suffering for the good of the saints. "For you." (See v. 13; Col. 1:24.)

   a. Not a prisoner for crime, debt, or war captive but a prisoner for his service to the church. Willing to suffer rejection, even imprisonment for the people he loved and was called to serve. Christ suffered for the church.

      b. Paul's sufferings allowed him to enter into Christ's sufferings for the church. If you love the Lord and serve the church, you will suffer.

CONCL: Suffering conforms us to the image of His Son! Suffering teaches us dependence on God alone! Suffering perfects in us Christlike patience! Suffering shatters the kingdom of self and makes us mindful of others! Suffering dresses us for the place He has gone to prepare for us!

Paul's life tells the unbroken story of living martyrdom. Five times he received 39 lashes. Three times he was beaten with rods. Imprisonment, stoning, shipwrecks, fasting, hunger, thirst, sickness, cold, nakedness. These things made him look the part when he called himself "a spectacle unto the world" (1 Cor. 4:19). At conversion, he was told what things he must suffer, not what benefits he would receive. His life ended by execution at Nero's guillotine. But this age is more interested in medals than scars.

Christ has called us to: a cross, not a cushion; a pilgrimage, not a picnic; a fight, not a frolic; an execution, not an excursion. Death to self, to sin, to the world. (See 2 Tim. 2:12; 2 Cor. 4:17.)

ILL: There are no sharp stones on the sands of the seashore. Even broken bits of glass and shells lose their cutting edge on the beach. Pebbles are rounded. Why? Attrition, irritation does it. Ceaselessly, the waves roll one edge against another, till all are worn smooth. A rough experience, but it grinds off all their ragged corners. That is what the waves of adversity do to human lives. Round out character. Remove rough edges. Trouble teaches. Trials train. People who have lived long and known adversity are the easiest to live with. Their cutting edges are gone.

II. THE MYSTERY OF THE CHURCH

"How that by revelation he made known unto me the mystery;
(as I wrote afore in few words, Whereby, when ye read, ye may
understand my knowledge in the mystery of Christ)." (3:3–4)

Ephesians 3:2–6

INTRO: Ephesians presents the church in several analogies.

It is likened to: a Body (1:23); a Kingdom; a Family, Temple (2:19–21); a New Man (4:13, 24); a Bride (5:25); humanity/society, Soldier (6:11).

Here in ch. 3 it is likened to a mystery. The word "mystery" recurs 3 times in this chapter: vv. 3, 4, 9.

"Mystery" is repeated 6 times in the epistle: 1:9; 3:3–4, 9; 5:32; 6:19.

"Mystery" Gr: MUSTERION "to shut the mouth, silence, secret." In the NT a mystery is not the mysterious or the unknowable. It is a particular part of God's plan known to Him from the beginning, and withheld from man's knowledge until God's special time to reveal it. It is that which is outside the range of unassisted natural understanding, and can be known only by divine revelation. Sacred secrets. Spiritual mysteries. Divine silence.

There are several sacred secrets in the Scriptures, such as the mystery of Christ's indwelling (see Col. 1:26–27); of God's incarnation (see 1 Tim. 3:16); of Israel's rejection (see Rom. 11:25); of iniquity (see 2 Thess. 2:7); and of the rapture (see 1 Cor. 15:51–55).

The greatest of the sacred secrets is the mystery of the church. The OT prophets did not see the church age. They prophesied Christ's coming to set up His Kingdom, but not to establish His church. The grace period was a spiritual mystery hidden from them. Kept secret in ages past but revealed at God's special time by His Spirit.

The mystery of God's will is that He purposed in eternity past to gather together divided, fragmented humanity into one body, the church through Christ. A body of particular members who care and share together. One with God. One with himself. One with others. Only in the church through Christ can the alienation, fragmentation, and polarization be remedied. Man is unified and made one. So when Paul uses "mystery," it describes something unknown to man BC, but now revealed fully. In this passage some wonderful disclosures are made concerning The Mystery of the Church.

A. Grace is Its Origin (v. 2)

1. The Dispensation of God!

    a) LIT: "assuming (taking for granted the fact) that you have heard." This was not a personal determination, but a dispensation of God. "Dispensation" Gr: "administration, economy, stewardship."

    b) Not a period of time, but a manner of dealing or arrangement of administration of affairs.

    c) God had favored Paul with the message of all men's inclusion in the church. This was God's special arrangement, a way of dealing.

2. The Dispensation of Grace!

    a) It was the dispensational age of the church.

    b) It had to do with the dispensational privileges of the Gentiles. A period of God's grace. Something unknown before now.

    c) The message of God's grace brought by the messenger who had been given administration of the grace of God to the Gentiles. (See 1 Cor. 9:17.)

B. Known by Revelation (vv. 3–4)

1. "Revelation" Gr: "to fling aside or draw back the veil." Making known that which was before concealed from view or knowledge.

2. Natural Revelation!

a) Some things all men can know. The unregenerate man can know God's existence through nature. They can know God is powerful through creation.

b) However, other things God reveals by His Spirit only to His special people.

3. Special Revelation

a) The truths which Paul proclaimed to the Gentiles were not derived from any human source. Not intellectual deductions of his own mind. Not the spiritual intuitions of his own personality. They were revealed to him by God. (See Gal. 1:11–12.)

b) In the OT they had the spoken revelation by the prophets. In Bible Times they had the Living Revelation in Jesus Christ. In our day we have the Written Revelation of Scripture. In the OT, "He reveals His secret unto His servants the prophets" (Amos 3:7).

c) In the NT all God's people have access to the same secrets of God's Word. Nothing added, nothing taken away, the Scriptures are God's final revelation. (See 1 Cor. 2:14; Matt. 11:25.)

d) The mystery (secret) of Christ (word, church) is revealed to God's people by His Spirit.

C. Hidden from Ages Past (v. 5)

1. The Secret Hidden by God!

a) The purpose of preaching (v. 9)

b) It is the mystery "which in other ages was not made known unto the sons of men."

c) Not a mystery in the sense of being incomprehensible, but in the sense of being undiscovered by men because it was unrevealed by God. It was unrevealed therefore unknown by men in past generations. The whole gospel was once a mystery because it was in the mind of God as an idea, but unrevealed to the universe.

2. The Secret Revealed by The Holy Spirit!

    a) We are privileged to know what the OT prophets did not know.

    b) They wrote about them and desired to know what was written but could not know them.

    c) In fact, we know what the angels cannot know. (See 1 Pet. 1:10–12; Rom. 16:25–26; 1 Cor. 2:7–10; Matt. 13:10–11, 34–35.)

D. Explained in Detail (v. 6)

1. The chief thing Paul wants to say about the mystery of God's creating one new people in Christ is that all people hold their salvation blessings jointly in God's church.
2. The structure of the grammar here is striking.

    a) Paul uses three parallel, composite expressions.

    b) In the Gr. these words each begin with the prefix SYN, "together with."

    c) There is no way to capture the precise force of this usage in English.

    d) KJV: "fellowheirs, and of the same body, and partakers of his promise."

    e) PHILLIPS: "equal heirs with his chosen people, equal members and equal partners in God's promise."

    f) NIV: "heirs together with Israel, members together of one body, and sharers together in the promise in Christ Jesus."

3. All Believers Are Fellow Heirs Together of God!

    a) Heirs together with Israel. Not heirs after but together with. Not attached to Judaism, but joined together within one body.

    b) We enjoy the privilege of children. (See Rom. 8:17.)

    c) These words embrace all that a person receives and will receive in salvation. It is the whole of God's blessings possessed jointly by all believers. No inner-circle recognized.

No preference realized. No first-rate/second-rate. But jointly-equal-fellow-together with.

d) All believers are fellow-members-together of one Body!

   1) The idea here is the mystical union possessed by God's people in the church.
   2) Each member equally important to the body. (See 1 Cor. 12:13; Col. 3:11.) No differences, distinctions!

e) All believers are fellow-partakers together in the promise! "The promise" not the promises plural. "The promise" of redemption, made to the first pair in Eden, repeated to Abraham, which is the subject of all OT prophesies. (See Gal. 3:14, 19, 22, 29.)

CONCL: The mystery-secret is now revealed. God is gathering together all alienated, fragmented humanity into one body, the church. Now the church is no mystery. God's secret is known to all who will know it. So God's church is no mystery. What is a mystery to me is that I, even I, was included in God's new society, the church. That I can be a functioning member of the Body of Christ. That I can be a fellow-citizen in the Kingdom over which God reigns. That I can be a part of the Temple in which God dwells. That I can be a son in the family of which God is our Father. Paul never got over the wonder of the great doctrine of the church, nor that he had been chosen to make it known to his world. The revelation of the church is no less ours as it was his. We also bear the responsibility to share with our world what God is doing.

ADDITIONAL SCRIPTURES: The Mystery of the Church

1. The Mystery of Christ's Indwelling! (See Col. 1:26–27.)
2. The Mystery of Divine Incarnation! (See 1 Tim. 3:1.)
3. The Mystery of Israel's Rejection! (See Rom. 11:25.)
4. The Mystery of Iniquity! (See 2 Thess. 2:7.)
5. The Mystery of the Rapture! (See 1 Cor. 15:51–55.)

We are privileged to know what OT prophets did not know! (See 1 Pet. 1:10–12; Rom. 16:25–26; 1 Cor. 2:7–10; Matt. 13:10–11, 34–35.)

We are fellow-partakers together in the promise! (See Gal. 3:14, 19, 22, 29.)

III. THE MAKING OF A MINISTER

"Whereof I was made a minister, according to the gift of the grace of God given unto me by the effectual working of his power." (3:7)

Ephesians 3:7–8

INTRO: Here is a brief sketch, short summary of a true gospel minister. He is the subject of vicarious suffering (v. 1), intense, voluntary, and Christlike. He is the recipient of Divine revelation (vv. 2–6), sacred secrets, grand truths, and spiritual mysteries. This passage (vv. 7–13) describes him as the messenger of redemptive mercy.

Having explained the mystery of the church as God reveals it by His Spirit, how that God through Christ is gathering together all humanity into a new humanity, the church. How that in the church all believers are fellow-heirs together of God. No exclusiveness, no exclusions. How that all believers are fellow-members together of one body. No distinctions, no differences. How that all believers are fellow-partakers together in the promise of redemption made by God to all mankind without exceptions.

Now in this paragraph he deals with the making of the minister for the preaching of the mystery. It is fitting to follow the mystery of the church with the making of the minister. The church is the vehicle of God's redemptive mercy. The minister is the messenger of God's redemptive mercy. This passage shows the man, the message, and the meaning of preaching the mystery.

A. The Minister of God (v. 7)

Here are traits which mark a God-made minister:

1. A True Minister is God Made. (The one absolute fact.) "Whereof I was made a minister" Gr: DIAKONOS.

   a) The basic meaning is servant. In particular a servant who waits on tables. NT deacon. It later came to refer to servants in general.

b) By definition, a servant is one who acts on command of another, one who recognizes and submits to higher power. Primary responsibility is to do what he is told to do. Paul means here he became one who ministered the gospel, and served God in that capacity.

c) There are no assembly-line ministry factories. Ministers cannot be mass-produced like hot house plants. They are not man-made by seminaries, or well-meaning relatives and friends. They are not self-made by their own ingenuous, inherent human abilities. They are God-made and Heaven-sent. Now there are two essentials in their making.

2. A Minister is Made By The God-Given Grace of a Divine Call

a) "According to the gift of the grace of God given unto me."

b) Not earned, nor learned, but given to me by the grace of God. The office Paul held was a gift by the grace of God. He was no self-styled, self-appointed preacher.

c) He did not make himself a minister. He was "made a minister." It was not a chosen vocation. Not a personal choice but a Divine calling.

d) Paul's call was as real as his conversion on the Damascus Road.

e) There on his back in the road, he heard God's call. (See Acts 26:16; Col. 1:25.)

3. A Minister is Made By The Dynamic Anointing of God's Spirit! "By the effectual working of his power."

a) "Effectual" Gr: "in working, divine operative power, Spirit's energy working within." The anointing of God's Spirit.

b) TR: "by the energetic working of his power."

c) It was not Paul's fine education, nor natural abilities, nor human experience, nor charismatic personality, nor great flu. Not any such thing could qualify him as a minister.

d) No man can preach the gospel effectively in his own strength and power. He may talk eloquently, but talk is not preaching. It will lead to nothing. Spirit energized for effectiveness.

That is the only thing worthy to be called preaching. (See 1 Tim. 1:12; 1 Cor. 2:4; Col. 1:29.)

B. The Message of the Gospel (v. 8)

1. The Mission of Proclamation! "Preach among the Gentiles."
2. Primacy of preaching. (See 1 Cor. 1:21; Titus 1:3.) "Manifested His word through preaching."

   a) "Among the Gentiles" which were outcasts of society. The right attitude, "Less than the least of the saints."

   b) The memory of his past life and the thought of the calling to preach Christ drove him to a sense of his own unworthiness. A minister who does not feel himself "the least of all saints" is not likely to become the greatest of all preachers.

C. The Message of Christ!

"The unsearchable riches of Christ." What a profound phrase—sublime statement. The business of the ministry. The mission of the church.

1. The "unsearchable riches" is Christ Himself. Not what He has to give us. Christianity is Christ.
2. Everything is in Him. God has treasured up all His riches in His Son. The riches of His glory—His grace—His rich mercy. Without Him we are nothing. So the "unsearchable riches" are all the riches of Christ Himself and the whole wealth of salvation which He gives. (See John 1:16; Col. 2:2–3.)
3. They are indeed "unsearchable" by human efforts.

   a) "Unsearchable" Gr: "that which cannot be traced out."

   b) If we could only see what is in Christ for us. His riches are so vast they cannot be searched out by human exploration. Untraceable. Riches so unlimited, sufficient, and abundant that they cannot be fully explained, expressed, or explored by human efforts alone. "Unsearchable." Only the Spirit can lead us to what we need at the time we need it. (See Phil. 4:19.)

c) What are some of the "unsearchable riches" of Christ? Although cannot be fully described, a few can be mentioned. What is there in Christ for any one of us at any moment?

d) ILL: Look at it this way. I am poor—empty handed—a pauper. What do I need? Christ has everything I need. But what are the things I need most? The answer is given: see 1 Cor. 1:30.

4. Christ is made unto us wisdom! I can know God. IN HIM is the wisdom and understanding of the great perplexing issues: such as God and man; life and death; purpose and destiny.

5. Christ is made unto us righteousness! I can be forgiven. IN HIM I am made right with God and can stand before God in righteousness.

6. Christ is made unto us sanctification! I can live right. IN HIM the sanctified life is possible; I can continue to live a clean, sanctified life pleasing to God. Growing spiritually.

7. Christ is made unto us redemption! I can be glorified. IN HIM I can expect complete salvation (spirit, soul, body). He will raise my body, change it, and glorify it.

CONCL: So in Christ I can draw on the unsearchable riches! Wisdom—I can know God! Righteousness—I can be forgiven! Sanctification—I can live right daily! Redemption—I can expect complete salvation, including a new body. We have only scratched the surface of His unsearchable riches. Do you know the treasure of God's grace? Are you drawing on these riches? Are you enjoying the riches, the unsearchable riches of Christ Himself?

ILL: Many church people are like the Laodiceans, who thought they had everything and needed nothing. To them it was religious routineness, church as usual, ho-hum spirituality. Their attitude is expressed in no uncertain words (see Rev. 3:17). Then the Glorified Christ said to them: "Buy of me gold tried in the fire, that thou mayest be rich" (Rev. 3:18). There is no reason to be spiritually bankrupt. There is no reason to be spiritually poverty stricken. Unsearchable riches of Christ are in reach of each believer. There is a price to pay. The move is yours.

IV. MANIFESTING OF THE MYSTERY

"And to make all men see what is the fellowship of the mystery, which from the beginning of the world hath been hid in God, who created all things by Jesus Christ." (3:9)

Ephesians 3:9–13

INTRO: This passage is a continuation of the ministry to make known the message of the gospel. Indicated by the first word, "and." We come now to God's eternal purpose in manifesting the mystery of Christ and the Church. It shows how God is manifesting the wisdom of the ages to men and to angels. This paragraph follows Paul's description of the minister of God and his primary responsibility, the proclamation of the gospel of God—the unsearchable riches of Christ. The manifestation of the eternal wisdom of the ages is portrayed here in two streams of thought.

A. Divine Purpose in Manifesting Wisdom (vv. 9–11)

1. Illumination of men! (v. 9)

   a) The Divine purpose is the illumination of darkness. Spiritual darkness is prevalent.

   b) Darkness is caused by spiritual blindness. (See 1 Cor. 4:3–4; Eph. 4:18; 2 Cor. 4:6; Eph. 1:18.)

      1) "To make all men SEE." That word does not adequately translate the word the Apostle used. Gr: "to illuminate—to impart light—to shed light upon."

      2) Illuminate: turn the lights on in the mind and heart.

      3) Turn men's ears into eyes so they may see the eternal plan of God concealed from the beginning, now revealed in the gospel of Christ.

      4) The purpose of preaching is to illuminate the minds of men as to God's eternal plan kept secret from the

foundation of the world. Make known "the fellowship of the mystery."

    5) "Fellowship" is an unfortunate trans. Gr: "plan, administration, stewardship, carrying out," of God's wisdom of ages.

    6) The light which Paul had been given and was to shed to all men was that God has a plan, a purpose for this world. God has a plan for the whole of man, the whole of life, and the whole of history.

2. Instruction of Angels! (vv. 10–11)

    a) "The manifold wisdom of God" Gr: "many-sided, variegated, multiformed, many-colored."

    b) Our great salvation and the glorious church are the final and supreme manifestation of God's wisdom.

    c) The supreme purpose of the church is to glorify God by manifesting His wisdom before the angels, who then offer greater praise.

    d) The angels can see: the power of God in creation, the wrath of God at Sinai, the love of God at Calvary. But above all, they see the manifold (multi-colored, multi-faceted) wisdom of God made known through the church.

    e) In the classroom of God's universe: He is the Teacher; the angels are the students; the church is the illustration; the subject is the manifold wisdom of God.

    f) Why the Angels? When Satan and the fallen angels rebelled in eternity past, God could have annihilated them forever. That would have been just and reasonable. It would have eliminated Satan from the fall of man after the creation.

    g) That would have demonstrated His power, but not His mercy.

    h) God in His own infinite, perfect wisdom already had an eternal plan to create a new humanity, the church, the plan of redemption in Christ.

    i) God knew Satan would seduce man from his righteousness and cause him to fall into misery. And also He knew Satan would think he had won.

j) But while Satan is turning the human race against God and setting human beings against one another and even against themselves, God is at work by His Holy Spirit, creating a new people, the church. A people who will glory in doing right, even when it is not popular; who will delight in pleasing God, even when they suffer for it.

k) So let the drama of history unfold, manifesting the manifold wisdom of God while the angels in the heavenlies are constantly praising God for His perfect, infinite wisdom.

l) So God has a plan for the whole of history, the whole of man, the whole of life. (See v. 11.)

m) Then all Heaven will recognize the wisest thing God ever did is to bring all men together into one body, the church through Christ.

B. Human Privileges from Manifestation (v. 12)

1. The gospel has brought us believers two great privileges:

   a) We Have BOLD ACCESS to God!

      1) "Boldness" Gr: "fearlessness, freedom from all apprehension, a freedom from any doubt that we may be rejected or denied entrance."

      2) ILL: A bold man is one who steps straight forward, who is afraid of nothing. Though he faces a mighty enemy, the bold man walks with shoulders squared and head high with confidence and assurance. He knows no inhibitions. He is not hesitant, doubtful, nor uncertain. Boldness is the exact opposite of anything that indicates weakness.

      3) "Access" Gr: "entrée." It means a way of getting in, a means of entry. It speaks of the privilege of entrance, of admission where others are not allowed.

      4) It refers to our relationship with God in Christ whereby we are acceptable to God and are assured He is favorable towards us. He looks with favor upon us. He is waiting

to receive us. We do not have to hesitate at the doorstep. We have a right of entry, an access, an entrance.

5) We can without fear or apprehension approach God in the trying times of life and find grace to help in time of need. (See Heb. 4:16.)

b) We Have CONFIDENT FAITH in God.

1) We know, no matter what happens, God is still in charge of His world, and that the eternal plan is right on schedule.

2) "Confidence" is always the end of a process. It means you have been practicing something so diligently that now you are confident in respect to it.

3) ILL: Like learning to ride a bicycle. The first moment the hand of the one teaching you was taken away, you were hesitant, uncertain, and frightened. However, after riding several times you soon gained confidence. You were ready to ride alone without assistance. You had developed confidence. (See Heb. 10:19–22; 1 John 5:14–15.)

CONCL: The phrase "by the faith of Him" influences the whole verse. In whom and through faith in Him denotes our union with Christ and the power by which it operates. We know, no matter what happens in the world, no matter the circumstances of our life, God is still in charge of His world and our lives, and the eternal plan of God is right on schedule. Faith is that sixth sense.

ILL: If you only knew what I know! The story is told of the father who put his young son to bed one evening and sat down to finish the paper. Later he noticed a sound coming from his son's room and a light under the door. He walked to the door and stood still for a moment. He heard his son laugh and say, "If you only knew what I know." He repeated the phrase again. Finally the father went in and asked the son to explain. "Well, Dad, I was just reading a few pages in my storybook before going to sleep. When the plot thickened and things looked bad for my hero, even apparent defeat and death, I just could not put it down and did not have time to finish the book. So I just turned over to the last chapter and read the outcome. Sure enough, the villain was destroyed and the hero triumphed. Then as I continued to read a few pages, I could not help, when the hero got in trouble, to stop and laugh, 'If you only knew what I know.'"

Part 2: THE MINISTRY OF PRAYER (3:13–21)

V. THE PINNACLE OF PRAYER

"For this cause I bow my knees unto the Father of
our Lord Jesus Christ, Of whom the whole family
in heaven and earth is named." (3:14–15)

Ephesians 3:14–19

INTRO: Paul's prison prayers are unique! He prays for others, not himself. He centers on spiritual blessings, not on material or physical needs. This takes us to the preacher's place of prayer. It pictures the preacher on his knees before God for church. "I bow my knees." Not just the bended knee. It is the Eastern prostration with the head touching the ground between the knees, a mark of deep reverence. Here is prayer at its highest expression! It is indeed the Pinnacle of Prayer. The summit of prayer, for there is no place higher. The highest point, zenith, apex. He prays for their Spiritual Enablement. Never has more been asked of God than in this one-sentence prayer. In the original text these five verses form only one sentence. But what meaning and significance is packed and pressed into that sentence!

Four burdens seem to weigh heavily on the prayer's heart:

1. The POWER of God's Spirit upon them! (v. 16)

2. The PRESENCE of God's Son within them! (v. 17a)

3. The PRACTICE of God's Love among them! (vv. 17b–19a)

4. The PERVASION of God's fullness in them! (v. 19b)

The word "THAT" seems to divide the prayer into four petitions. Petitions of intercession which describe the spiritual needs of the church:

A. The Strengthening of the Spirit (v. 16)

1. This strengthening is an endowment of riches!

    a) "Grant you": Expect nothing from God but a free grant. You do not earn it, merit it, borrow it, pay it back. It is a free grant from the riches of His grace. "According to the riches of his glory": Giving is done according to ability. Receiving is done according to capacity. ILL: See Matt. 9:29. God gives "according to," not just "out of" His riches.

    b) ILL: Disgrace for a King to give no more than a peasant. TR: "In proportion to the wealth of His glorious resource."

    c) ILL: A king had given a most generous gift to a relative and came under severe criticism. His reply, "Let the whole world know that when the King gives, he gives like a King."

    d) ILL: A poor subject came to King for assistance. He was touched and gave liberally. "Your Majesty, this is too much." King's reply, "It may seem too much for you to take, but it is not too much for me to give."

2. This strengthening is an enduement of power!

    a) "Strengthened with might" TR: "a mighty increase of strength." A double explosion.

    b) LIT: "empowered with power." "Might" Gr: DUNAMIS: English equivalent "dynamite," meaning explosive power, earth-moving force.

    c) "His Spirit in the inner man" ILL: It is like a hand and glove: Believer is the glove. Holy Spirit is the hand. The glove yields to the hand.

    d) ILL: See Judges 6:34. TR: "The Spirit of the Lord clothed Himself with Gideon." (See 2 Cor. 4:16.)

B. **The Indwelling of Christ (v. 17a)**

1. This makes religion a matter of the heart, not the head; from facts to experience. Not just recognition of a God in heaven, but receiving Christ into the heart. ILL: An analogy of the believer to a temple built up for a habitation of God through the Spirit. Evidently a reference to Solomon's Temple, where the Shekinah Glory of God dwelt.

   a) Christ indwelling is by faith! Saving faith admits Him. Sanctifying faith submits to Him.
   b) Christ indwelling is in love! "Dwell" Gr: "down home" means to "move in, settle down, and feel at home" in the believer's heart and life. (See Gal. 2:20; Col. 1:27; Rev. 3:20.)

C. **The Knowing of Love (vv. 17b–19a)**

1. The most deprived man in the world is the one who does not know love—mother, father, family, companion, friend. The love of Christ is the basis for all human relationships. "Know" Gr: "to experience"!
2. It is the beginning of Christian life! "Rooted and grounded in love." ILL: Double illustration. One of agriculture, the other of architecture. Soil of love. Foundation of love.
3. The understanding of His love!
4. "May be able to comprehend."

   a) Full comprehension of believers.
   b) "Comprehend" Gr: KATALAMBANO, "to take eagerly, seize possessingly, grasp hold of." Apprehension not enough.

5. Full dimensions of God's love. Love's four dimensions signify its greatness.

   a) ILL: Science of divine dimensions. God's love is like a cube, the perfection of form. From every side it is a perfect square. At any angle it is the same appearance. The Holy of Holies a cube; New Jerusalem a cube.

b) See Job 11:8–9. "Breadth" universal embracing all—wide as wide! "Length" infinite from everlasting to everlasting—long as long! "Depth" unfathomable stoop to lowest hell—deep as deep! "Height" heavenly reaching beyond gravity—high as high!

6. The experience of His love!

a) "To know the love of Christ, which passeth knowledge." It is surpassing human knowledge. It is not knowing the unknowable. It is to know that love which surpasses human knowledge of love. Beyond human knowledge. It is the knowledge of the heart!

b) ILL: A baby satisfied in mother's arms. You reach for it. Holds tighter. You persist. Baby screams: "I don't know you; I don't know whether you love babies or not. I know my mother's love. I trust her. You leave me alone."

c) What does a baby know about the love of mother? Does not understand reasons for. Yet it definitely knows the love of mother. This kind of love surpasses knowledge.

D. The Filling of Fullness! (v. 19b)

1. "Filled" Gr: complete, fully equipped like a ship ready for voyage! NT usage of "filled" means controlled by. Here the prayer reaches its highest expression, "filled with all the fullness of God."

a) To be "filled with . . . God" is a great thing!
b) To be "filled with . . . the fullness of God" still greater!
c) To be "filled with all the fullness of God" is utterly incomprehensible.
d) ILL: Like dipping a cup full of lake water. That cup is not all of the lake. But it is the fullness of the lake. It contains ingredients of water of the lake. The fullness of the lake is in the cup of water.

2. We never have the totality of God, but all His attributes are in us in small measure, such as love, goodness, mercy, holiness, power, so that we are indeed "filled with all the fullness of God."

CONCL: Here the prayer reaches the place where it becomes praise. He is so engrossed and lifted up in the spirit of prayer he just overflows into praise (vv. 20–21). We have seen here how Paul has risen from petition to petition, and from height to height, until he reaches the absolute pinnacle of prayer—"To be filled with all the fullness of God." Beyond this there is nothing more one could desire in prayer. For nothing greater could happen to any of us than "to be filled with all the fullness of God." Having asked for that, having prayed for that, there is nothing more that one could do. There is no further prayer. Nothing more available. No greater blessing.

VI. THE TRIUMPH OF PRAISE

Ephesians 3:20–21

INTRO: All believers have experienced the burden of prayer; the struggle of intercession; the joy of thanksgiving. Need to discover the triumph of praise. Praise is the highest form of worship to Almighty God! Petition is asking God for things we want or need. Intercession is pleading with God on behalf of others. Thanksgiving is gratitude to God for what He does. Praise is extolling and adoration of God for Who He is. Somewhere in the struggle and burden of prayer, Paul reaches the high plane of triumphant praise.

Here the preacher is in the place of prayer for his church. Paul's prison prayers are unique: Always for others, never himself. Always for spiritual blessings, never material things or physical needs. Four burdens seem to weigh heavily on the pastor's heart (vv. 16–19):

1. Power of God's Spirit upon them—The strengthening of the Spirit (v. 16)

2. Presence of God's Son within them—The indwelling of Christ (v. 17)

3. Practice of God's love among them—The knowing of love (vv. 17b–19a)

4. Pervasion of God's fullness in them—The filling of fullness (v. 19b)

There has never been more asked of God than in this one-sentence prayer. Paul is unconscious of the boldness of his praying.

This beautiful doxology of praise closes Paul's prayer for the church. He is so engrossed and lifted up in the spirit of prayer that he just overflows into triumphant praise: "Now unto him that is able. . ." This doxology of praise says three things about God to help us discover The Triumph of Praise:

A. Declares the Sufficiency of God's Ability (v. 20a)

His praise seems to bypass the thought of asking too much or going beyond God's sufficiency. Expression falls short of it. The man on his knees has risen into the rapture of praise; the cry of exaltation; the true song of triumph. He is lifted to the place in prayer where God's sufficiency came into view. To this point he saw only human need. But now he saw God's ability to answer prayer and supply human need. He makes this declaration clear in two ways:

1. By Building A Pyramid Of Power! He is able to do EXCEEDING ABUNDANTLY ABOVE ALL that we ask or think. And all this, "according to the power that worketh in us."

2. By Revealing The Measure of His Ability!

   a) "Exceeding abundantly" Gr: HYPEREKPERISSOU, "vastly more than more, immeasurable." Another of Paul's coined words.

   b) Here language is strained to the limit: trying to speak the unspeakable; define the indefinable; measure the immeasurable.

   c) Put in human terms the illimitable, the absolute! See how he piles words one on top of another. Man's need can never overtake God's bounty and grace!

   d) ILL: Fill a glass so full it cannot hold another drop. That's "all that we ask." Gr: "fullness."

   e) Continue to pour into the glass until it overflows. That's "above all that we ask." Gr: "OVER-fullness."

   f) Now keep on pouring until the overflow drenches the floor. That's "exceeding abundantly." Gr: "EXCESS BEYOND OVER-fullness."

   g) So God fills our little measure to overflow, then pours upon the overflow, and still upon the flow of the overflow He continues to pour.

   h) ILL: Powerful statement, "Exceeding abundantly above all." Strong superlatives showing excessive sufficiency of God's power. (1) "Above all"—EXCESS! (2) "Abundantly above all"—EXCESS OF AN EXCESS! (3) "Exceeding abundantly above all"—EXCESS OF AN EXCESS OF AN EXCESS!

   i) The grammar here is superlative of superlatives in force. In good old American English, Paul says, "God is able to do super-abundantly above and beyond what we ask or think, and then some on top of that."

      1) God is able to do ALL we can ask or imagine!

      2) God is able to do MORE THAN we can ask or imagine!

      3) God is able to do IMMEASURABLY MORE than we can ask or imagine!

B. Describes the Working of God's Power (v. 20b)

  1. We Have The Power!

    a) The word "power" here is Gr: DUNAMIS, Eng: dynamo, dynamic, dynamite. Inherent, stored-up power.

    b) We have power in us: Holy Spirit, Christ, Divine love, the fullness of God.

  2. The Power That Works!

    a) "Worketh" Gr: ENERGIA, "energy, energize."

    b) ILL: How it works—Romans 8 describes the spiritual life of believers. Begins "no condemnation" (v. 1); ends no separation in the Spirit // in Heaven; Justification ends glorification. In the course of living that life: WE NEED HELP—AN INTERCESSOR! (See Rom. 8:22–23, 26.)

      1) Three groans:

        a. Creation groans (v. 22);

        b. Believers groan (v. 23);

        c. The Spirit groans (v. 26).

      2) The Holy Spirit in us does the office work. He never leaves the office; collects and classifies the documents; and arranges the evidence.

a. The Son of God in Heaven goes to court and pleads our case before the Judge and jury.

b. This is intercession within and intercession on high! The Spirit of God in the heart with unutterable groaning, breathing out to God our needs. The Son of God on high takes these trembling words and purifies them of human defect, then presents them before the throne of God as a perfect prayer worthy of an answer. This is "the power that worketh in us."

C. Discloses the Eternality of God's Glory (v. 21)

1. This Glory is "Unto Him" Alone!

   a) Here is the focus of praise. God alone is the focal point of praise and glory in the church. It is beneath our dignity to share this glory with anyone/anything else.

   b) Our tribute, To God Be The Glory! For every miracle. For every soul. For everything.

2. This Glory is "In The Church."

   a) Our purpose is a ministry of praise. Nothing gives such glory to God as does the church (v. 10).

   b) All creation proclaims His glory. The mountains, the rivers, the raging sea, the lightning/thunder all proclaim His glory. (See Ps. 19:1.)

   c) But there is nothing that proclaims the glory of God like the church. Its creation, its existence, its makeup is nothing less than miraculous. That we who were wicked and evil in the world, we who were lost and dead in sin and trespasses, could become members of the Body of Christ. It took a miracle.

3. This Glory is "By Christ Jesus."

   a) And through Him.

b) The Son glorifies the Father, and we being in Him, and in His church, also minister glory to God. To glorify God is our purpose:

    1) By Offering Praise (See Ps. 147:1.)
    2) By Good Works (See Matt. 5:16.)
    3) By Fruit Bearing (See John 15:8.)
    4) By Spiritual Unity (See Rom. 15:6.)
    5) By Entire Dedication (See 1 Cor. 6:20.)

4. This Glory is "Without End."

a) LIT: "Unto Him be glory in the church by Christ Jesus in all the generations of the age of the ages."

b) You cannot add to that! "All the generations" of what? Of the age of the ages. What is the age of the ages? It is the age of the ages, age upon age upon age, world without end! Forever and ever. Eternally!

    1) Elders at the Throne (See Rev. 4:11.)
    2) Heavenly Host (See Rev. 5:12–13.)
    3) Angels and Elders (See Rev. 7:12.)
    4) Hallelujah Chorus in Heaven (See Rev. 19:1, 5–7.)

ADDITIONAL NOTES:

ILL: He is a God of the excess!

God's sufficiency is expressed in terms of "excessive" as it relates to human need.

1. When God supplied manna to Israel in the wilderness, it came in boxcar-load quantity daily. More than enough daily supply for one million people. (See Ex. 16:15–35.)
2. When God supplied oil to the bankrupt widow, there was more than enough to fill every available vessel. (See 2 Kings 2:1–7.)
3. When Jesus fed the multitude of 5,000-plus with 5 loaves and 2 fishes, there was more than enough, with 12 baskets full of leftovers. (See Matt. 14:17–20.).
4. When life gets difficult, believers are assured, "We are more than conquerors through him that loved us" (Rom. 8:37).
5. When the times are sinful, we are told, "But where sin abounded, grace did much more abound" (Rom. 5:20).

❖ Chapter 4 ❖

VOCATION:
THE CHRISTIAN WALK
—UNITY AND PURITY

Ephesians 4:1–32

INTRO: The life of the church is compared to a walk of faith. Christian faith is both a matter of the head and of the heel. Here faith is moved from the sanctuary to the sidewalk, from the study to the street, from precept to practice, from sitting at Jesus's feet to following in His footsteps.

Part 1: WALKING IN UNITY (4:1–16)

I.   THE WORTHY LIFE (4:1–3)

    A. Weighty Words (v. 1)

    B. Worthy Ways (vv. 2–3)

II. THE UNITY OF THE SPIRIT (4:4–6)

    A. The Unifying Work of the Holy Spirit of God (v. 4)

    B. The Unifying Work of Christ the Son of God (v. 5)

    C. The Unifying Work of God the Father (v. 6)

III. CHRIST'S GIFTS TO THE CHURCH (4:7–12)

    A. All Believers Have Gifts (v. 7)

    B. Christ is the Giver of Gifts (vv. 8–10)

C. Gifts are for Divinely Specified Purpose (vv. 11–12)

IV. GROWING IN DISCIPLESHIP (4:13–16)
    A. Growing in Simple Christlikeness (v. 13)
    B. Growing in Spiritual Stability (v. 14)
    C. Growing in Christian Genuineness (v. 15)
    D. Growing in Body Ministry (v. 16)

Part 2: WALKING IN PURITY (4:17–32)

V. BEING A NEW MAN (4:17–24)
    A. The Walk of the Old Man (vv. 17–19)
    B. The Walk of the New Man (vv. 20–24)

VI. LIVING A NEW LIFE (4:25–32)
    A. Change from Lying to Speaking Truth (v. 25)
    B. Change from Sinful Wrath to Righteous Anger (vv. 26–27)
    C. Change from Stealing to Sharing (v. 28)
    D. Change from Vile Language to Wholesome Words (vv. 29–30)
    E. Change from Natural Vices to Spiritual Virtues (vv. 31–32)

Part 1: WALKING IN UNITY (4:1–16)

I. THE WORTHY LIFE

Ephesians 4:1–3

INTRO: This passage is an appeal on the basis of the good doctrine just explained (chs. 1–3) to live The Worthy Life.

Vv. 1–3 are a preliminary statement which prefaces the worthy life addressed here in two aspects: unity among believers (4:1–16), and real-life relationships (4:17–32).

Ephesians, like most of Paul's epistles, is divided into doctrinal and practical sections. The great doctrine of the church is explained in chs. 1–3. Its heavenly origin from eternity past revealing God's redeeming love to us "before the foundation of the world." Its earthly formation from degenerate humanity to become the masterpiece of divine workmanship. Its spiritual edification through the ages toward the accomplishment of God's grand design to "gather together in one all things in Christ."

Chapter 4 is the transition point! "Therefore" is the pivotal word! It points backward to the doctrine of the church. It leads forward to the life of the church. He had just painted the awe-inspiring portrait of the glorious church without spot or wrinkle. He had piled up before their eyes all the golden wealth of their privileges in Christ Jesus. Now in black and white he draws a picture of the possibility of human failure. Considering their high calling and considering the depths of possible compromise, there is emotion in the plea (v. 1). Then he proceeds to give us a beautiful picture of The Worthy Life:

A. Weighty Words! (v. 1)

Paul uses five strong words here to convey some powerful ideas:

1. "Prisoner" Conveys The Idea of Cost!

a) He begins this appeal by identifying himself as "The prisoner of the Lord." A gentle reminder that the worthy life can be costly. He had paid considerably for his obedience to the Lord.

b) He was "the prisoner of the Lord" whether in jail or not. What Paul says: "Live as I live. I am living the life of a prisoner. I am actually in prison at this moment. I am in prison because I do not decide what I do. I am the servant of Jesus Christ. I am His bond slave. My loyalty to Christ cost me my liberty. I am in prison because of the gospel message that I believe and preach. I am not in charge of myself. I am in His charge." (See 1 Cor. 6:19.) We have no right to live as we choose and as we please.

2. "Beseech" Conveys The Idea of Choice!

a) Not a demand or command. Not a request or suggestion. He pleaded with them. He was a leader, not a driver. They must follow by choice.

b) "Beseech" Gr: PARAKALEO "to entreat, to call to one's side with the idea to help or be helped." He had just entreated God on behalf of the church. Now he entreats the church on behalf of God. It carries intense feeling, strong desire. But the choice was personal.

3. "Walk" Conveys The Idea of Lifestyle!

a) "Walk" Gr: "a way of living before men, a manner of life, his earthly walk, his lifestyle." This is not a worldly walk, but it is an earthly walk.

b) Here the Christian life is compared to a walk of faith. It is a matter of head, heart, and heel. Attitude, consecration, and conduct.

c) Here faith is removed from precept to practice, sanctuary to sidewalk, study to street; from sitting at Jesus's feet to following in His steps. Christian faith is authenticated by your walk. Both how you walk and where you walk. (See 1 John 1:7.)

d) ILL: A poor man who could neither read nor write was handed a gospel tract. He asked, "What is this?" When he was told it was a tract, he replied, "Well, I can't read it; so I'll just watch your tracks." The greatest short sermon any Christian can hear.

4. "Worthy" Conveys the Idea of Balance!

   a) "Worthy" Gr: "to have the weight delicately balanced." The idea is the scales of life in which the weight on one side always equals the weight on the other. In this case, the weight of practice equaling the weight of doctrine.

   b) A second idea, "becoming of," such as dress in color/appearance. Human behavior must always be worthy of the divine calling. Character and conduct must always match confession and creed. Works must match faith. We are called to walk on a plane commensurate with the gospel. (See Phil. 1:27; Col. 1:10; 1 Thess. 2:10.)

   c) ILL: A citizen is obligated to abide by the laws of the country. An employee is obligated to work according to the rules, standards, and purposes of his company. Members of special groups are obligated to promote the goals and abide by the standards of the group. So the Christian is obligated according to the rules, the standards, and the purposes of the gospel. Balance is the idea: not all doctrine but equal practice. Not all practice but equal doctrine. Without both, we become lopsided and unbalanced.

5. "Vocation" Conveys the Idea of Calling!

   a) "Vocation" Gr: KLESIS "a calling." Vocation, not vacation! KJV renders "vocation," but "calling" is better.

   b) In contemporary speech, "vocation" has come to mean something we choose, while "calling" is something for which we are chosen. How exciting to think of life as a calling of the Lord. "Church" Gr: EKKLESIA "the called-out ones." There are two parts of this calling, which deserves special notice:

1) Called from darkness to light! (See 1 Pet. 2:9.) We were blind and in the dark before conversion.

2) Called from death to life! (See Eph. 2:5; 1 John 3:14.)

B. Worthy Ways! (vv. 2–3)

There are five traits of the worthy life in these verses:

1. Humility—"Lowliness!" (v. 2)

   a) "Lowliness" used only one other place in the NT (see Phil. 2:3). Gr: "humility, modesty, lack of pride and self-assertion."

   b) Humility is a Christian word. Paul probably coined it. There was no Greek word for it. Everyone knows a Christian should be humble.

      1) Humility is the opposite of pride and self-assertion. We are saved by grace through faith, not by works (see 2:8–9). No human pride or boasting allowed. Not easy to do.

      2) Pride is so easily wounded by what we consider thoughtless, unfair conduct of others.

      3) ILL: Chinese rice farmer. Third-tier rice patty. Humility does not insist on personal rights; puts the interests of others before its own.

2. Gentleness—"Meekness!" (v. 2)

   a) "Meekness" only 8 times in NT.

   b) Gr: "gentleness" or power and passion under control; gentled to the point we can live and work together without hurting each other.

   c) ILL: The same Gr. word was used of wild horses tamed to the point of working with men without danger.

   d) Meekness is too often today misunderstood. To most, meekness suggests weakness. But that is not the idea at all.

      1) ILL: Meekness was the chief trait of Moses (see Num. 12:3). But Moses was not a weak man. He was a strong man. Strong enough to appear before Egypt's Pharaoh (see Ex. 8:1).

2) ILL: The Lord Jesus was meek and gentle, yet strong (see Matt. 28:29; Matt. 5:5).

3. Patience—"Longsuffering!" (v. 2)

   a) "Longsuffering" Gr: means to endure with unruffled temper or it is patience.

   b) It takes time to learn patience. Patience is learned chiefly through suffering.

   c) ILL: Pious church member and pastor. (See Rom. 5:3.) We acquire patience through the things we suffer. Longsuffering is a valid translation of "patience" for it simply means suffering long.

      1) It is what God does with us.

      2) Therefore, we ought to suffer long, be patient, with each other.

4. Love—"Forbearing!" (v. 2)

   a) Forbearing love is another form of patience, but it is different. This one relates directly to trials we have as a result of uncharitable conduct towards us by another person.

   b) Our attitude is love, not retaliation. Endure the wrong. Suffer the slight.

   c) Thus we demonstrate a way of life superior to that of the world.

   d) "Forbearing" used only one other time in the NT (see Col. 13:13). Gr: "to put up with."

5. Unity—"Peace!" (v. 3)

   a) It is the unity of the Spirit. Unity which the Holy Spirit gives. Not created by the church or man-made.

   b) It takes human effort to maintain. Not easily kept for endeavor means diligence.

   c) We can't build it, create it, make it. All we can do is "keep it."

   d) "Endeavoring" Gr: "giving diligence; earnestly striving."

CONCL: This unity of the Spirit is the bond of peace. It is the bond that is peace. We are bound together and united by the Holy Spirit. We have all been born of the Spirit, filled with the Spirit, and led by the Spirit. All the signs of the worthy life that Paul enumerates here result in peace: humility, gentleness, longsuffering, forbearing love. Conversely, pride, arrogance, and selfishness separate and divide. Each of the four virtues depends upon getting self out of the center. And that makes for peace, individually and collectively. Christians are "born from above" and exhibit character traits which are "high born." We are above some things because of our new nature, such as pride, arrogance, selfishness, and hatred.

II. THE UNITY OF THE SPIRIT

Ephesians 4:4–6

INTRO: This practical section of Ephesians begins with a discussion of the Christian lifestyle. It speaks first to the individual believer, who is to walk in humility and gentleness (v. 2).

Then it widens to include the entire church which is to walk in perfect harmony (v. 3).

It is the unity of the Spirit. This is a proper name referring to the Holy Spirit, not the human spirit. It is the unity which the Holy Spirit creates. This unity is created by the fact that we are all born of the Spirit, filled with the Spirit, and led by the Spirit.

It is not the unity of man for a human purpose. Not man-made. Not created by man nor by the church. It is the creation of God. Yet it requires human effort to maintain. We are told to diligently KEEP it. We can't build it or create it. All we can do is keep it.

This passage (vv. 4–6) deals entirely with the unity of the church. The language structure of these verses emphasizes the significance of biblical numerics relating to unity.

Biblical numbers are important here. The entire statement is only one sentence. There is a sevenfold repetition of the word, "ONE" (vv. 4–6).

"One" in the Bible is a symbol of unity. "Seven" is the number for perfection or completeness.

It is also interesting how the seven ones are grouped:

A. The 3 in v. 4 relate to the Holy Spirit.

B. The 3 in v. 5 relate to Christ the Son.

C. The 1 in v. 6 relates to the one God and Father of all.

The unity begins with the one body and finalizes with the unity that is God Himself.

In this passage, Paul names seven basic spiritual realities in three specific groupings that unite all true believers.

A. The Unifying Work of the Holy Spirit of God! (v. 4)

The first set of three speaks of the work of the One Spirit grafting us into the one body and giving us that one hope.

1. There is One Body of Christ!

    a) "One body" speaks of the mystical, universal, invisible church. It illustrates a unity of diversity (see 1 Cor. 12:12).

    b) The apostle is asserting that there is only one true church. It consists of all those who are truly born again of the Spirit of God.

    c) The church spans all cultures and all centuries. It is the one body of Christ with many and different members. Yet one body. This is clearly a great argument for preserving the church's unity. Based on what we are: one body. We suffer divisions at great loss.

2. There is One Spirit of God!

    a) "One Spirit" speaks of the Holy Spirit of God and His great work in us. It illustrates a unity of experience.

    b) Paul says, "You are one because of the one work of the one Holy Spirit." (See 1 Cor. 12:13.)

    c) We sometimes speak of the uniqueness of our personal experience of conversion. But the one Spirit did the identical work of salvation in all our hearts. The work of conviction, conversion, regeneration, and sanctification.

    d) The one Spirit marvelously and miraculously unites us in a common experience.

3. There is One Hope of Calling!

    a) "One hope" refers to our common hope of heaven because of our high calling. It illustrates a unity of destiny.

b) We are all traveling towards the same destination. The Bible's idea of hope means "sure and certain." In the world, it means something uncertain, cannot really expect it.

c) Human ideas of the future often divide the church.

d) But this one hope unites the church in the sure and certain expectancy of Christ's coming, the resurrection of the body, and a home in heaven.

B. The Unifying Work of Christ the Son of God! (v. 5)

The second group of three speaks of the work of the one Lord who revealed the one's faith that leads us to one baptism of identification with Him.

1. There is One Lord of Heaven.

   a) "One Lord" refers to the unique Lordship that belongs to Jesus alone. It illustrates the unity of service or servanthood.

   b) The nearest thing to a creed in the NT church is Phil. 2:11. (See also Acts 4:12.)

   c) He is the same Lord to all who submit to Him. Some say, "That's not the Jesus I know—I don't know that Jesus."

   d) There are not many lords. There is only one Lord.

   e) If we follow and obey this one Lord, He will be a force for drawing us together.

2. There is One Faith That's True!

   a) "One faith" speaks of the content of the faith that is contained in the gospel. It illustrates the unity of the truth.

   b) The faith as revealed by Jesus Christ. It is not faith that brings salvation, but the faith which is the content of the gospel. Christ is its object.

   c) Not a faith, but the faith! (See Jude 1:3.)

   d) This one faith binds us together so we can stand shoulder to shoulder before the world and give a united testimony of God's saving work in Jesus Christ.

3. There is One Baptism in Christ!

    a) "One baptism" speaks of the singular outward testimony of the inward experience of salvation. It illustrates the unity of identification.

    b) Baptism must never divide Christians. Its significance is identification with Christ. That is the unifying thing.

    c) Are you baptized into Christ? That is the work of the Holy Spirit. Water baptism is the outward sign of the inward work of the Spirit.

    d) Identified together with Christ as Savior, we stand together for Him.

C. The Unifying Work of God the Father! (v. 6)

Finally this great passage comes to a tremendous crescendo which draws an awesome picture of God. The final one of the sevenfold unities in this Trinitarian passage culminates in the ascription of ultimate unity to God the Father. It illustrates ultimate unity of all things. The word "ALL" recurs 4 times. Four is the Bible number for creation, suggesting here that all created order finds its completeness and perfection by being joined to God within the church. This verse says four things about our "One God":

1. He is The Father of All!

    a) It begins with the paternal love of God as our Father.

    b) The greatest truth about God is not that He is King of Kings, the mighty Creator, Supreme Being, Eternal Judge, but that He is Father.

2. He is ABOVE ALL!

    a) God is pre-eminent.

    b) He is transcendent.

    c) He is above all creation.

    d) He is not dependent on His creation.

3. He is Through All!

   a) Here is the providence of God. God is operative in His world. He is at work. He is still in control.

   b) God did not create the world and set it going like a man might wind up a play toy and leave it to run down.

   c) God is throughout His world, guiding, sustaining, and working.

4. He is IN All!

   a) This shows the Presence of God. God is imminent. He is in the universe.

   b) He gives order to our world. He adds meaning to life on this planet.

   c) To the Christian, we live in a God-created, God-controlled, God-sustained, God-filled world.

CONCL: The unity of God is inviolable. So is the unity of the church. The oneness of the church is undeniable. It is the one body into which God is bringing together into one all divided, separated, and fragmented humanity. God wants us to be one. One in His church. That oneness is based on individual believers living a life of humility. Humility in turn produces meekness (gentleness), which produces longsuffering, which produces forbearing love. On that basis alone we can keep the unity of the Spirit in the bond of peace. Then the world can look at the church and say, "They are different . . . they are supernatural." We may win them to faith in Christ and the church without saying a word. Are you with him? Do you have it all together? At one with God, with others, and with yourself?

ILL: A pastor told the story of visiting a home, and the members of the family were asked to quote Bible verses.

One little girl quoted John 3:16 like this:

"For God so loved the world, that He gave His only begotten Son, that whosoever believeth in Him, should not perish, but have INTERNAL life."

The pastor did not correct her. Indeed it is INTERNAL life as well as ETERNAL life.

III. CHRIST'S GIFTS TO THE CHURCH

Ephesians 4:7–12

INTRO: The average church today has a serious unemployment problem. Not of people looking for work. But of work looking for people. This kind of church is much like a football game. Let me explain:

ILL: The great athlete Bud Wilkinson was a part of the President's Physical Fitness Program. He was asked during an interview, "What contribution does pro sports make to the physical fitness of America?" To no one's surprise, he replied, "Very little. For example, a pro football game is happening where 50,000 spectators, desperately needing exercise, sit in the stands watching 22 men on the field desperately needing rest."

That's a typical modern-day church. A host of spectators, and a handful of participants. It has been determined that in an average church of 100 members, 5 are actively engaged in the work of the church while 95 are willing to let them do it.

In such a church individual Christians are impoverished, and growth is stunted.

This passage gives us God's remedy for this serious spiritual problem. The practical section of Ephesians begins by calling the believer to exemplify the traits of the Spirit. A worthy life is characterized by a humble attitude, gentle disposition, patient suffering, and forbearing love.

Then it continues to show us a oneness of the Spirit, a bond of peace shared by all the body of Christ.

Now in this passage (vv. 7–12), he points toward the gifts of the Spirit by which every member is enabled to effectively do the work of the church. This text makes four powerful statements about gifts:

A. All Believers Have Gifts! (v. 7)

1. Uniqueness of each member. The word "BUT" is a contrast word. LIT: "in spirit of that on the other hand." It is used to contrast the unity of ALL believers with the uniqueness of EACH believer.

2. The gift of each!

   a) The gift here is called a "grace." Gr: CHARIS from which charismatic derives. It is a capacity for service given to every true Christian without exception. Something which he did not have before salvation.

   b) ILL: Paul's personal testimony (see 3:8). Clearly, one of Paul's gifts was preaching (see 2 Tim. 1:6).

   c) This is the uniform testimony of Scripture. Explicitly stated, and clearly implied. (See 1 Cor. 12:7, 11; 1 Pet. 4:10; 1 Cor 12:28.)

   d) The church is made up of "gifted members." The gifts are distributed by God and are designed to make the body complete. If the church is to be effective, each member must discover his gifts and begin exercising them in some spiritual ministry.

   e) A large number of these spiritual gifts are dormant, unrecognized, and unused. So the church suffers.

B. Christ is the Giver of the Gifts! (vv. 8–10)

1. A Quotation From Psalms! (v. 8) (See Ps. 68:18.) With application to the ascension of the Risen Lord, who upon His return to heaven gave gifts to His people.

2. ILL: This was a war song, a victory hymn, written and sung in celebration on the occasion of some great victory of a military conqueror. The conqueror is represented as returning in triumph; parading through the Holy City of Jerusalem; and ascending up Mt. Zion, the Hill of God. Lavish gifts from the spoils of victory were generously distributed. They would display the King's own soldiers who had been freed after being held captive by some enemy. Often referred to as recaptured captives.

3. With the Battle of the Ages won at Calvary, verified by the power of His resurrection, Heaven's conqueror, the King of Kings, ascends to the eternal Hills of Glory, triumphant over Sin, death, and hell. By that victory over Satan, the Prince of Glory recaptured those captive to sin and gave gifts for the welfare and development of His church.

4. Parenthetical Statement! (vv. 9–10)

   a) Here he shows how this victory song is applied to Christ.
   b) He that ascended, "FIRST" descended (came down to earth).
   c) He that descended (incarnation) "ALSO" ascended (Return to Heaven's glory) . . . that He might fill all things.

C. Gifts are for Divinely Specified Purpose! (vv. 11–12)

1. Observe two great truths here:

   a) The Gifts of Ministry! (v. 11)

      1) These are not intended as a system, order, ranking of ministry. They are not just offices within the church, but gifts of God to edify the church.
      2) God's gifts are to individuals for the whole body: the gift of apostle-izing prophesying; of evangelizing; of pastoring; of teaching.
      3) He in turn gives these "gifted men" to the church.
      4) The office cannot function effectively without the gift. Apostles are "SENT OUT" to men in special need! Prophets "SPOKE OUT" the message of God to men! Evangelists "GAVE OUT" the gospel to the unconverted! Pastors/Teachers "WATCH OUT" as shepherds for the total welfare of the flock of God.

   b) The Ministry of Gifts! (v. 12) Note the threefold progression in the development and growth of the body of Christ.

      1) Gifted ministries equip the saints!

         a. "For the perfecting of the saints . . ." Gr: equipping, maturing, completing, preparing.

b. The basic idea of the word is that of putting a thing into the condition in which it is usable. (Mending, restoring, preparing.)

c. To see that the members of the church are so informed, so guided, so cared for, so sought for when astray, that they become usable to one another in building the body.

d. Equipping saints is the first priority in a growing church.

2) Prepared saints do the work of ministering!

a. "For the work of the ministry . . ."

b. TR: "The wording of this ministering . . . business of service."

c. The idea here is practical service. The wording of this passage indicates that it is not the leaders who have the most direct responsibility in the business of service.

d. No pastor can do all that needs to be done in a church.

e. God's plan is for the equipping to be done so that fully prepared saints can serve each other effectively.

f. Members grow by feeding on the Word; by ministering to each other.

3) Effective ministering builds the church!

a. "For the edifying of the body of Christ."

b. "Edifying" Gr: "building up, constructing, development, growth."

c. It is a construction term referring to building of house.

d. Derivation of English "edifice," a large. imposing building.

e. It is the "body of Christ" that is built up. Not the preacher's ego. Not the church's pride. Not personal kingdom building. Not great cathedrals or facilities.

     f.   The building-up of the church is linked to the Word: hearing, learning, obeying.

CONCL: All God's children have gifts. A new capacity for service. A supernatural enabling for Christian service. The gifts are the power source for effective service.

ILL: Spiritual gifts are like so many electrical appliances. What a variety of appliances are available today. Electric toasters, toothbrushes, mixers, irons, razors, dishwashers, and on and on. Someone said they saw an advertisement for an electric shoestring tier. I may be ready for that one myself in a few more years.

Look carefully; though they are vastly different in size, appearance, and function, there is one thing they all have in common. They all have a cord and plug at the end. They are all designed to utilize the same power. To operate, they must be plugged in at the power source.

The power source for spiritual gifts is the Holy Spirit. Pentecostal power. So many Spiritual Gifts in this local church lay dormant, unrecognized, unused. How can I know, recognize, discover my gift? How does a member of the human body know its place and function? How does it discover its capability anew? function? It receives its orders from the head.

Five sure steps: (1) It is initiated by prayer. To leap over this step is to stumble and fall on your face. (2) It is enlightened by study. Scriptures expose us to the gifts of the Spirit. (3) It may be indicated by desire. (4) It will be confirmed by ability. (5) It will be accompanied by blessing.

IV. GROWING IN DISCIPLESHIP

Ephesians 4:13–16

INTRO: Christ commissioned His Church, "Go, preach, teach, and make disciples." (See Matt. 28:19–20.) So the mission/purpose of the church is discipline.

In my early Christian life, three things happened to me in this process of discipline:

1. I made up my mind to serve the Lord, no matter what happened. I made a firm decision for Christ. No matter about family, friends, or anything else. The only matter was, I will serve the Lord.
2. God saved me. I got an old-time, life-changing experience of salvation. No one had to tell me, you are saved now, just claim it. You are forgiven, just accept it. When I left that altar, I had something I knew about and wanted to share with others.
3. God gave me a good, godly pastor. My first and only. A pastor who spared nothing in disciple-making. Through a good example, and great portions of God's Word, he disciplined, matured, mended, prepared, and helped me find my place in the Body of Christ.

Now this is the Divine plan:

1. God gifts individual believers with special gifts of ministry; and in turn gives these gifted persons to the church to perfect, mend, mature, and equip the saints, so that in turn (first objective),
2. Those disciplined, prepared, equipped individual believers may do the work of ministering to other body members, so that in turn (ultimate objective),
3. The body of Christ may be edified and built up, growing in the grace and knowledge of God.

We are in a body-building program in this church. Each and every member of this local body is important/essential to the progress of the church, the process of growth. Now the passage before us today defines four critical areas of spiritual growth in which the church must be making progress: Christ-likeness! Spiritual stability! Christian genuineness! Body ministry!

A. Growing in Simple Christlikeness! (v. 13)

Here are three ways to grow in Christlikeness:

1. Doctrinal Integrity

    a) The unity of the faith is doctrinal integrity. It means getting it all together regarding Bible doctrine.

    b) This is not faith as an act of believing. It is faith as the body of Christian doctrine. THE FAITH is the content of the gospel in its most complete form.

    c) A believer is growing in Christlikeness when he has a shared understanding of the great truths revealed in the gospel.

2. Personal Relationship

    a) "Knowledge" means getting it all together in our ongoing personal relationship with Christ. It does not refer to salvation knowledge.

    b) It is a deeper experience, fuller knowledge of Christ that comes only from study of the Word and prayer.

    c) It is a growing encounter with Jesus Christ. Coming to know Him more and more, directly and personally. A relationship which is deepened and enlarged with each experience.

    d) A believer is growing in Christlikeness when he has a dynamic, ongoing, personal, spiritual relationship with Jesus Christ.

3. Ultimate Maturity

    a) The goal of maturity is "a perfect man" and defines him as "the measure of the stature of the fulness of Christ."

    b) "Perfect man" Gr: means mature manhood, fulfilling our humanity, being all that God intended when He made man in the beginning.

    c) A whole person, a complete human being, grown up, responsible, well-adjusted, wholehearted person like Jesus.

d) A believer is growing in Christlikeness when there is a continual striving for ultimate maturity in Christ.

e) Understanding the gospel, knowing Christ, reaching toward maturity. That's Christlikeness, a growing experience for all.

B. Growing in Spiritual Stability! (v. 14)

1. The Christian is admonished, "Be no more children."

   a) "Children" Gr: "one who does not talk," infancy, babyhood.

   b) Contrast between childlikeness and childishness. Childlikeness is that refreshing simplicity of faith which just believes God and obeys without question. Childishness is that erratic attitude which tends to infantile behavior, immature reactions, and emotional outbursts.

   c) Here are two characteristics of childishness:

      1) Demonstrated by Instability of Behavior!
         These unsettled, vacillating believers are like an unmanned boat, bobbing up and down, veering here and there, controlled and tossed about by changing erratic winds.

         a. They are fickle, changeable, jumping from one thing to another, carried about by every changing circumstance, forever riding the crest of some new religious fad/trend. Unfaithful! Undependable! Unreliable!

         b. This childish instability retards spiritual growth.

      2) Characterized by Gullibility in Judgment!

         a. They are extremely naive. Unaware of danger.

         b. Undiscerning of a threatening situation.

         c. Easily convinced by innocent-sounding false teachings.

         d. Being mentally gullible, they are unaware that false teachers practice clever trickery. That it is deceitful, unscrupulous scheming to mislead the religious naive.

C. Growing in Christian Genuineness! (v. 15)

1. It means possessing what one professes!

   a) "Speaking the truth" Gr: means LIT: "trusting it." Conveys the idea of walking in a true way. It means truthing it as opposed to faking it.
   b) ILL: Youth expression: "Get real!"

2. It means sincerely living the Christian life!

   a) This verse means more than just speaking. It is believing and living genuinely.
   b) Being real and authentic as opposed to pretentious.
   c) Hatred of hypocrisy which is masked play-acting.
   d) Development of honest, realistic attitudes demonstrated in daily life.
   e) Real love produces spiritual genuineness in life.

D. Growing in Body Ministry! (v. 16)

Here is Scriptural church growth: development of spiritual cohesion, and coordination among members. Fitted. Compacted. Cooperating. Ministering. Increasing. Growing!

1. The Church is a Body with Many members!

   a) Each member has a particular function for the well-being of the whole body.
   b) At conversion God places each member into the body with a specific function or ministry to perform for the good of the entire body. (See 1 Cor. 12:28; 1 Pet. 4:10.)

2. The Dynamics of Growth are Resident in the Body!

   a) This verse pictures the church as a dynamic, growing organism. Each member doing what it was placed in the body to do causes growth to the body, the building up of itself in love.

b) The church is illustrated by a human body.

c) ILL: It consists of various and different members, united by joints and ligaments; each part being proportioned to its place, and enabled for its service; the whole body being compacted by the nerves, and circulation continually going on from the heart through every part of the body.

d) Thus it grows to maturity with every member performing its proper function, in union with the Head, and in perfect harmony with all other members for the common good of the whole body.

CONCL: The entire church grows as each believer grows in discipleship toward spiritual maturity. (See 2:10.) Each Christian is God's glorious handiwork. Personal creation. His masterpiece of workmanship. (See 1 Cor. 3:9.)

ILL: A building under construction, field under cultivation! In each the work is now in progress. Will continue to completion.

ILL: An admirer asked Rembrandt at what point a painting was complete. "When it expresses the intent of the artist." Under construction until it expresses God's intent for human beings: A PERFECT MAN!

ADDITIONAL NOTES: Growing In Discipleship!

Growth is continual! For the Christian the old life is constantly coming to an end, and the new life beginning. This is why Paul said, "I die daily" (1 Cor. 15:31).Which was only another way of saying, "I am continually growing." Growth is natural! No laws have to be passed to keep grown-up men and women from riding stick horses and making mud pies. See vv. 13–16. The analogy presented here is that of growth and development from infantile babyhood through unstable adolescence on to mature manhood.

Life's changing viewpoints:

—the old believe everything!
—the middle-aged suspect everything!
—the young know everything!

ILL: In most any machine shop there is a tracer lathe. It has an air-controlled "finger" that traces its way along a fixed template. The template is the exact pattern of what is to be turned out on the lathe. As this sensitive little finger follows along the template, its every movement causes the tool cutting the product from the lathe to make a precise replica of the template. That is God's specialty. He places His finger on the template, and thereby creates His own workmanship in believers. At times the tool bites in, causing the heat to increase because of friction. We squirm and may even try to get away. But the Father holds us tightly to the lathe of His will. His goal is that we bear the image of His Son. We are His workmanship.

ILL: (See Hos. 14:5.) A pastor once preached a stirring message on Growth in Grace, after which one of the members approached him and said, "You have gotten to my heart recently and I've been trying to 'grow in grace' for some time, but it seems I'm not getting anywhere." The preacher pointed to a tree, "Do you see that tree?" Wondering reply, "Yes." The Pastor continued, "Well, it had to be planted before it could grow. Likewise you must be 'rooted and grounded in Christ' before you can begin to grow spiritually." It hit him like a bomb. He fell down at the altar and wept his way to a real experience with Christ.

ILL: (See Hos. 14:6.) Have you ever noticed that the trees nearest the light at the edge of a forest have larger branches than those deep in the woods? The same tree will throw out a long branch toward the light, and a short one toward the darkness and obscurity of the forest. So a man grows toward the light to which he turns. He grows according to the direction in which he turns with greatest affection. If it is the bright lights of the world, he grows worldly. If it is toward the great Light of the world, he grows Christlike, nurtured by the sunlight of His love.

ILL: A little girl coming in from the flower garden with soiled hands, dress, and shoes. She was a mess, making a clever observation: "Mother, I know why flowers grow; they want to get up out of the dirt." Believers grow upward and onward to higher altitudes.

Part 2: WALKING IN PURITY (4:17–32)

V. Being a New Man

Ephesians 4:17–24

INTRO: There is still a difference! When a person is genuinely saved, a transformation takes place in his basic nature. This change is more basic and radical than the change that will take place at death.

ILL: When a Christian dies, he is already fitted for heaven, already a citizen of the Kingdom, already a child of God. He simply experiences perfection of the divine nature because for the first time he is free from the unredeemed flesh. The future receiving of his glorified body will not make him better. It will only give him full capacity for all that eternal resurrection life involves.

But salvation is not a matter of improvement, or perfection of what has previously existed. It is a total transformation. A basic transition. A radical change.

The NT speaks of believers as receiving: a new mind, a new will, a new heart, a new inheritance, a new relationship, new power, new knowledge, new wisdom, new understanding, new righteousness, new love, new desire, new citizenship. All which are summed up in the "newness of life" (see Rom. 6:4).

At new birth a person becomes a new creature. It is not that he receives something new, he becomes someone new. (See Gal. 2:20.)

The new nature is not added to the old but replaces it. The transformed person is a completely new "I."

Based on the fact that believers are new creatures, Paul makes two appeals (vv. 1, 17).

Then he contrasts the walk of the believer and unbeliever. It shows our proper response to being a new creature. That a changed nature demands changed behavior.

It literally says, "Since God has created a marvelous new being in the world called the church, and because of this unique creation, with its unique character of humility, its unique endowment with spiritual gifts, its unique unity as the Body of Christ, and its need to be built up in love, here is how every believer should live as a member of that church."

Now Paul moves to specifics, giving us characteristics of the walk of the old man, contrasted with the characteristics of the walk of the new man.

A. The Walk of the Old Man! (vv. 17–19)

This manner of life shows there is a difference.

1. In Intellectual Futility (v. 17)

    a) This ref. here is to the frivolous, empty aims in life. The unfixed, unsettled impulses. They were chasing shadows, blowing bubbles, doing anything to make time pass agreeably.

    b) They do not consider or know what they are, and where they come from nor where they are going.

    c) The basic issue of lifestyle centers in the mind. The use of such words: "understanding-ignorance-learning-teach mind-truth," all relate to the intellect.

    d) Because Christians and non-Christians think differently, they therefore act differently. In spiritual and moral issues the unbeliever cannot think straight. His rational processes are warped.

    e) Repentance is a change of mind. Salvation is called "a renewing of the mind."

2. In Spiritual Darkness (v. 18a)

   a) Blind to all that is spiritual. Ignorant of God, of the way of salvation. Even at best the natural understanding cannot discover spiritual things.

   b) It is made even more obscure than ever by sin. The mind is blind because the heart is bad. Men do not see the truth because they do not want to see it. The light that could lead them to God and righteousness is persistently shut out.

   c) It is a state of self-induced mental darkness. (See John 3:19.)

3. In Divine Alienation (v. 18b)

   a) Separation from real life. There is exclusion from the life of God. This darkness, ignorance, and separation from God are caused by their willful determination to remain in sin.

   b) Because men determine to reject Him, God's sovereignty determines to blind their minds, exclude them from His presence, and confirm them in their spiritual darkness. (See Rom. 1:28.)

4. In Sinful Depravity (v. 19)

   a) Spiritual insensibility "past feeling" lost the "ache" which should accompany wickedness. The phrase has been explained by the word "an aesthete." "Given" indicates voluntary treason. "Lasciviousness," depraved, dreadful acts. "Greediness," a desire of having more, cannot satisfy.

   b) They acquired a spiritual and moral callousness. "Blindness" Gr: "stone-marble-callous-petrify-harden." Sin is difficult to the beginner. There are barriers set up: a tender conscience, the warnings of nature, the teachings of Providence, the light of revelation, the examples of the good. These barriers have to be broken down.

   c) In the beginning, the sinner is arrested by remorse. But gradually the safeguards are neglected and despised until the habit is acquired of sinning for the love of sin.

   d) Recklessness follows. Restraint relaxed. Passions loosed. Until depraved indulgences become a way of life.

B. The Walk of the New Man! (vv. 20–24)

"But" is emphatic, showing a great contrast! "But as for you." You are not like that. You are changed. You are different. And what a difference.

1. You Follow A New Example! (vv. 20–21)

   a) The believer is represented as having "learned Christ." Not as having learned about him. But having reached a true knowledge of Him. Having heard His voice. Having been taught by Him. We know the truth in Jesus.

   b) Christ is our Mentor. He is our Teacher. He is the Truth.

   c) He restored to health our vain intellectual facilities.

   d) He brought us from darkness to His marvelous light.

   e) He bridged the alienation and reconciled us to God.

   f) He has healed us from sinful depravity, and we are saved. (See Matt. 11:28–30.)

2. You Have A New Experience! (v. 22)

   a) It is a crisis experience. A definite work of grace. A complete separation. A radical change. A total transformation. A spiritual revolution. Like putting off an old coat.

   b) The inward change is evidenced by outward conduct. The old man dies and is replaced by the new.

   c) ILL: A benevolent center sponsored a rehab program for homeless children on the streets of a big city. They were photographed when they entered. Then they were washed, clothed, and taught the basics. When they were sent out after learning a trade, they were photographed again. The change was marvelous. The photos were a reminder of what had been done for him.

3. You Are Now A New Man! (vv. 23–24)

   a) Here is how it happens in three steps:

      1) v. 22

        a. Many rescue missions have a "delousing room," where derelicts who have not had a bath in months discard their old clothing and are thoroughly washed and disinfected.

        b. The unsalvageable old clothes are burned and new clothes are issued.

    2) v. 23

        a. The change is not in the mind psychologically. It is not in a change of mental opinion.

        b. The change is in the spirit of the mind. That which gives the mind both its bent and its material of thought. Change the spirit of the mind and you renew (change) the mind.

    3) v. 24

        a. It is divine workmanship. A new creation in Christ.

        b. It bears an ultimate likeness after God.

  b) There are two major features of the new creation.

    1) It is created in righteousness.

    2) It is created in true holiness.

    3) Righteousness and holiness include:

        a. integrity, honesty, true, fair, open dealing, being just and true in every relationship:

        b. in the home and family, on the job, among neighbors, with strangers, everywhere and at all times.

        c. True holiness is the inside-out kind.

CONCL: This is a rags to riches story. From the rags of sin to the robes of righteousness.

ILL: In the OT, see Zech. 3:1–4. Some Christians (NT and now) somewhat resemble Joshua with rags of the old man still hanging about them. Ruining their appearance and certainly not becoming of regenerated children of God. There is a putting off! There is a putting on! That means a radical change! What a difference it makes! The new birth is described in the NT as:

1. A transformation from death to life! Total Transformation!
2. A transition from darkness to light! Complete Transition!
3. A change from the old to the new! Radical Change!

VI. LIVING A NEW LIFE

Ephesians 4:25–32

INTRO: Being a new man demands living a new life! The only reliable evidence one is saved is not a past experience of receiving Christ, but a present life reflecting Christ. (See 1 John 2:4.)

New creatures live like new creatures. New man—new life!

The admonition is positive. We are to put off the old! And we are to put on the new (vv. 22, 24)!

The born-again believer is represented as a new man. (See Ezek. 11:19; 2 Cor. 5:17; Gal. 6:15; Col. 3:10.)

The analogy is clear! The old man of sin is dead. A spiritual resurrection has brought forth a new man who is to pursue the new life. (See Rom. 6:4.)

This section lays down five specific changes (commands, principles) of the new life in Christ. They show the contrast between the old life and the new. Each is a negative counterbalanced with the positive.

A. Change from Lying to Speaking Truth! (v. 25)

1. The Right Message

    a) "Lying" Gr: Falsehood, the lie.

    b) Before you speak, be sure you have got it right. There is more than one kind of lie in the world.

    c) There is a lie in the speech. Sometimes deliberate. Sometimes almost unconscious. Truth demands a deliberate effort.

    d) There is also a lie of silence. It may be most common. Don't give silent approval to error. Speak up. Give warning. Even rebuke when necessary.

2. The Right Motive

   a) Right words for the right reason. Hold the truth sacred, because we are members of the same body.

   b) The body is safe only as senses and nerves pass true messages to the brain. Endangered when false messages are given.

B. Change from Sinful Wrath to Righteous Anger! (vv. 26–27)

1. Anger is Human (v. 26)

   a) Anger is not a momentary boiling-over rage, but rather a deep-seated, determined, settled conviction. Its NT use can represent an emotion good or bad, depending on motives and purpose.

   b) A nature on fire for truth and right must burn with indignation against wrong and cruelty. Righteous indignation. Anger at evil. Hatred of sin.

2. Wrath is Devilish (v. 27)

   a) Anger kills. Either the person who is angry or the one towards whom it is directed. Unforgiven anger develops into wrath. Bitterness. Resentment. Self-righteousness.

   b) Forgive quickly. Before the day is over. Don't give Satan an opportunity.

   c) Unforgiven anger opens opportunities for Satan to work.

C. Change from Stealing to Sharing! (v. 28)

1. Change of Former Practices

   a) "Steal" Gr: KLEPTO from which comes Kleptomaniac. Stealing is a basic flaw in human nature. We come into this world prone to steal. Even from the cookie jar.

   b) Quit taking what belongs to others. Respect the property of others.

   c) Good in quality. A God-honoring occupation. Honest employment.

2. Supplying of Others' Needs

    a) Honest hard work is good for soul and body. It does not mention work to support himself and family. That is natural.

    b) It does state work in order to have enough to share with needy. That is spiritual.

D. Change from Vile Language to Wholesome Words! (vv. 29–30)

1. Renounce Unwholesome Communication

    a) "Corrupt" Gr: "unwholesome, used of foul, rotten meat, vegetables or fruit." Unwholesome language is just as repulsive as a rotten apple or spoiled piece of meat.

    b) Off-color jokes, profanity, dirty stories, vulgarity, double meanings, innuendos should never cross our lips.

    c) This does not simply forbid injurious words, but puts a silencer on all that is not positively upbuilding/edifying.

2. Develop Wholesome Speech!

Three things about wholesome speech:

    a) It is good for edification. Builds up, helpful, constructive, encouraging, instructive, and uplifting.

    b) It ministers grace to the hearer. Gracious. Appropriate. Raw truth is seldom appropriate, and most often destructive. Saved by grace. Kept by grace. Live in grace. Speak in grace. The supreme character of God.

    c) It grieves not the Holy Spirit of God. Perhaps in nothing do we grieve the Holy Spirit more than by foolish, inappropriate, unprofitable speech. Or by listening willingly and without protest to idle gossip and backbiting.

E. Change from Natural Vices to Spiritual Virtues! (vv. 31–32)

1. Put Away A Bad Temperament! These Are Human Vices!

2. Possess a Good Attitude! These are Spiritual Virtues! Development of a positive Christian attitude:

a) "Kind"—Cultivate the quality of kindness, harshness only hurts

b) "Tenderhearted"—Allow yourself to feel for others. A good feeling for another. Callousness is damaging.

c) "Forgiving"—Practice the art of forgiving others. Be quick to forgive because you are forgiven. Let Christ's forgiveness to you prompt your forgiving. Treat others as you have been treated by Christ.

CONCL: The New Man received at conversion demands the New Life. Salvation is described as: a total transformation from death to life; a complete transition from darkness to light; a radical change from the old man to the new man. Therefore, we must put off the grave clothes and put on the grace clothes!

ILL: The raising of Lazarus from the dead perfectly illustrates this truth (see John 11). Lazarus died and was in the grave four days when Jesus arrived in Bethany. His sister Martha observed by now the decaying body smells. But Jesus spoke the Word, and Lazarus came forth alive from the dead.

A spiritual application of this truth is used in John 5:24.

Now note our Lord's next words in John 11:44. Take off the grave cloths! He is no longer in the world of death. He is now alive. Grave cloths are not appropriate any longer. Why wear grave cloths? Put off the old; put on the new!

Therefore, we must put off the rags of sin and put on the robes of righteousness!

ILL: God represents our self-righteousness as filthy rags. (See Isa. 64.) Someone says, "But he is such a good moral person." But there is a good that is not good enough! In God's sight. It is not our sins but our righteousness called filthy rags. "Rags" because they cannot cover us! "Filthy" because they only defile us!

Therefore, we must put off self-righteousness and put on Christ's righteousness!

ADDITIONAL NOTES: The New Life!

Sometimes it is difficult for the new man to live the new life in this old world.

ILL: I read the story of the little boy who went to the grocery and asked for a box of Tide detergent. The clerk asked, "Son, what do you need the detergent for?" The boy replied, "I want to wash my dog." The clerk said, "Well, son, that Tide detergent is pretty strong for washing a little dog." The boy said, "That's what I want." The clerk, "All right." And he sold him the Tide with the caution, "Now, you be careful when you wash your dog. That detergent is very strong; it might kill him."

The boy said, "I'll be careful." He took the detergent home. About a week later the little boy came back to the store and the clerk recognized him and said, "Son, how's your dog?" And the little boy replied, "I'm afraid he's dead." And the store clerk said, "Oh, I'm sorry, but I did try to warn you that that Tide was pretty strong to wash your dog with."

And the little boy shook his head and said, "I don't think it was the Tide that did it. I think it was the rinse cycle that got him."

Sometimes we survive the washing, but the rinse gets us.

It is easier, even fun to catch the fish. But it isn't any fun cleaning it.

Vv. 31–32: These two verses summarize all that has been said about the new life. And give us a formula for living a new life.

1. Look inward! Get rid of bitterness, wrath, anger, clamor, and evil speaking.
2. Look outward! Show to others kindness, compassion, and forgiveness.
3. Look upward! Receive forgiveness from God when you fail in the new life.

❖ Chapter 5 ❖

SEPARATION:
THE CHRISTIAN WALK
—LOVE, LIGHT, AND WISDOM

Ephesians 5:1–33

INTRO: This chapter continues the practical section of Ephesians under the analogy of The Christian Walk. Here we become followers of God walking in love, light, wisdom, and harmony.

I.   FOLLOWERS OF GOD (5:1–2)

    A. This is a Forgiving Love (v. 1)
    B. This is a Giving Love (v. 2b)
    C. This is a Living Love (v. 2a)

II. WALKING IN LOVE (5:2–7)

    A. List of Unmentionable Deeds (vv. 3–4a)
    B. Contrasts the Unmistakable Alternative (v. 4b)
    C. Warns of Unavoidable Consequences (vv. 5–6)

III. WALKING IN LIGHT (5:8–14)

    A. Light Produces Good Fruit (v. 9)
    B. Light Proves Good Conduct (vv. 8b, 10)
    C. Light Exposes Evil Deeds (vv. 11–13)

IV. WALKING IN WISDOM (5:15–20)

   A. Wisdom in Making the Most of Time (vv. 15–16)
   B. Wisdom in Understanding the Will of the Lord (v. 17)
   C. Wisdom of Being Filled with the Spirit (vv. 18–20)

V. WALKING IN HARMONY (5:21)

   A. Reverence for Our Father God (v. 21b)
   B. Respect for Our Fellow Christians (v. 21a)

VI. HARMONY IN MARRIAGE (5:22–33)

   A. The Submission of a True Wife (vv. 22–24)
   B. The Love of a Good Husband (vv. 25–33)

I. FOLLOWERS OF GOD

Ephesians 5:1–2

INTRO: The fifth chapter of Ephesians begins with one of the most startling statements of the NT. "Be imitators of God." It is the only place in the Bible where these words occur. What makes them so startling is that they point to a standard beyond which there is no other. It is the highest standard in the world. The sum total of all Christian duty. The Bible's supreme argument for holiness. The highest level of lifestyle. It is the ultimate ideal.

It is proposed by Christ Himself (see Matt. 5:45–48).

"Followers of God." What does it mean? Gr: MIMESIS "to imitate, to mimic, or to copy."

ILL: It was the main part in the training of a Greek orator in ancient Greece; the learning of oratory consisted of three things: theory, imitation, and practice. The essential part of training was the study and imitation of master orators gone before. So Paul insists, "Since you are training in life, you must imitate the Lord of life." Paul's argument is that children are like their parents. Sometimes this fact of life can be both encouraging and embarrassing to those who have children.

ILL: The closest American example of this imitation is when a boy copies the lifestyle of his dad so exactly that we say, "He is just following in his father's footsteps." Children resemble their father's physical features, qualities of spirit, and unconscious behavior. A child desires to imitate because he loves and feels loved. It is a dear relationship, parent-child. So we are to "walk in love" as dear children (see v. 1). The phrase "walk in love" shows that Paul chiefly has in mind the imitation of God's love. LIT: "Be constantly ordering your behavior within the sphere of love." This love is AGAPE love, which God is and which He demonstrated on the cross.

This passage points up three aspects of God's love which we are to imitate:

169

A. This is a Forgiving Love! (v. 1)

The imitation of God called for in this passage is definitely connected with the thoughts ending chapter 4.

1. The Imitation:

   a) Be kind as God is kind.
   b) Be compassionate as God is compassionate.
   c) Be forgiving as God is forgiving. The first part of God's love we are to imitate is His forgiving love.

2. We Are Forgiven. We Have Experienced Forgiveness!

   a) See 1 Cor. 6:9–11.
   b) The greatest evidence of love is undeserved forgiveness. God's love brought man's forgiveness.
   c) I was guilty as sin. But now I am forgiven!

3. We are Forgiving. We are To Practice Forgiveness!

   a) It is through knowing ourselves to be forgiven that we are set free to forgive others lovingly.
   b) People are in desperate need of forgiveness.
   c) ILL: A psychiatrist once said, "Most of what a psychiatrist does is directly related to forgiveness. People come to him with problems. They feel guilty about their part in them. They are seeking forgiveness. In effect, they confess their sin to the doctor and find that he forgives them. Then a pattern is established whereby they can forgive others in the problem."
   d) ILL: The director of a mental hospital once said, "I could dismiss half my patients tomorrow if they could be assured of forgiveness."
   e) That is what we have in Jesus Christ—forgiveness!
   f) Because we find forgiveness there, we can in turn be forgiving.

g) ILL: God's forgiveness is not a mere overlooking sin. As to say, "Well, people will be people. We'll overlook it for now. Just don't let it happen again."

h) God takes sin with such seriousness that He deals with it fully at the cross. And on that basis, Christ's death, we can know we are forgiven.

B. This is a Giving Love! (v. 2b)

The second thing about God's love we are to imitate is that it is a giving love! This giving love is both sacrificial and personal:

1. It is Sacrificial!

    a) God's love is the model of giving love and it is most clearly demonstrated on the cross.

    b) God has given us all things.

    c) However, the expression of the full measure of God's giving love is seen primarily at the cross. (See John 3:16; 1 John 4:10; Rom. 5:8; Gal. 2:20; John 15:13.)

2. It Is Personal!

    a) In the great passage Phil. 2:6–8, we are told that Jesus did not merely give up THINGS to save us but that He gave HIMSELF. He did not give up the things which were outward privileges of His Deity: The Glory of Heaven! The service of the Angels! The position of authority at God's right hand.

    b) See vv. 6–7. The heart of this passage is that Jesus gave HIMSELF to the point of even death.

    c) See v. 8. The greatest expression of love is not that it gives things or even that it gives up things, but that it gives ITSELF.

    d) ILL: A pastor related the story of counseling a couple who were having marital difficulties. The husband spoke in his frustration at one point, "But I don't understand it. I have given you anything a woman could want: a nice house, a good car, beautiful clothes. I've given you . . ." The list went on. At last the man ended and the wife replied, "Yes, John. That much is true. You have given me everything but yourself."

Why don't we give ourselves to other people? Because we are afraid and selfish. We want ourselves for ourselves. We are afraid of being hurt or disappointed.

C. This is a Living Love! (v. 2a)

The third thing our text teaches about God's love which we are to imitate is that it is to be a living love. Forgiving! Giving! But also Living! It occurs in v. 2 when Paul says, TR: "And live a life of love, just as Christ loved us and gave himself up for us as a fragrant offering and sacrifice to God" (NIVUK). Living a life of love suggests two things:

1. It Suggests a Practical Love! If we ask, "What does it mean to live a life of love?" the answer is the very thing Paul has been saying in the previous chapter:

   a) Put off lying and speak truthfully.
   b) Put off anger and wrath.
   c) Put off stealing and do honest work.
   d) Put off unwholesome talk and speak to help others.
   e) Put off bitterness, rage, anger, brawling, and slander, along with all malice, and instead be kind, compassionate, and forgiving. That is what it means to live a life of love.

2. It Suggests an Eternal Love!

   a) Living love suggests love that is made alive by the very life of God and is therefore an ETERNAL love, as God is eternal.
   b) Today love is weak and faltering, variable and unreliable. Our love needs the strong character of God's eternal love as described in Rom. 8:35–39.
   c) We can imitate that kind of living love if we look to God. Certainly not if we look at ourselves.

CONCL: We are to become "Followers of God." We are to imitate, mimic, copy. Mimic means to copy closely, to repeat another's speech, actions, or behavior. That is what we are to do with God. We are to repeat His actions, echo His speech, duplicate His behavior.

To do that we must spend time with God! Spend time with God in prayer! Spend time with God in the Word! Spend time with God in worship!

It is only by spending time with God that we can become like God. Like God in forgiving love, giving love, and living love.

LIT TR: "Be becoming therefore imitators of God, as children beloved, and be ordering your behavior within the sphere of love, even as Christ also gave Himself up on our behalf and in our stead as an offering and a sacrifice to God for an odor of a sweet smell."

ILL: In the British Museum, a Greek writing tablet, earlier than the Christian era, is displayed. It is the classical equivalent of a child's copybook. The headline has been written by the master. The scholar has copied the second with his eye upon the first. But afterward each line is a reproduction, not of the first writing, but of the last. Consequently, each line grows worse as it gets farther from the first line.

This is often the cause of the broken character of our lifestyle because we imitate one another. Reproduce our familiar imperfections. Instead of copying, imitating the likeness of the Master. (See 1 John 2:6.)

It's startling! It's staggering! Almost incredible. But here it is. "Be ye followers of God as dear children," better translated, "Become imitators of God, as children beloved."

ILL: Look at a little boy who loves his father and knows his father loves him. His greatest desire is to be like his father. He likes to sit in his father's chair. Tries to walk like his father. Tries to speak like his father. The father is the model. The child is the copy, the mimic. He is imitating his father the whole time. That's human nature, human love at its best. Now cleanse it and multiply it by infinity, and you discover what the Word is telling us to do. "Become imitators of God." Why? Because He is your Father!

II. WALKING IN LOVE

Ephesians 5:2–7

INTRO: I read of the disillusionment and frustration of those Christians who work closely with top political leaders in our nation's capital. One senator's aide remarked that the intentions of most are quite good! But whether they stand on the political right (conservative) or on the left (liberal), they are leaning to the view that neither one nor the other is able to solve our country's problems.

One senator said, "Not only don't we solve the problems, our legislation actually makes the problems worse." The Christians admit, "The real problem in America is a flaw in human nature which can be described as greed and lust."

This is not just a Republican, Democratic, Western bloc, or Eastern bloc problem. It is the problem of sinful humanity.

One cynical writer commented, "Under Communism man exploits man. Under capitalism the situation is exactly the reverse."

In Christ and the church, there is really a reverse because we become a new man, with a new nature, pursuing a new life. A new people living a new lifestyle.

In vv. 1–2, as children of God we are imitators of the forgiving, giving, and living love of God.

Now in vv. 3–7, as saints of God we are told what to avoid as we are walking (living) in love.

A. List of Unmentionable Deeds (vv. 3–4a)

1. We Are Saints! "As becometh saints."

    a) We are saints and there is a difference. Saints and sinners are not alike. Saints are what we are.

    b) Doctrine is what we believe.

c) Righteous is how we behave.

d) Made saints at the new birth.

e) Separated unto God, and from sinful humanity.

f) Called saints because of our sanctity.

g) Something about us makes men think of God. When the world sees how you live, they learn something about God.

h) ILL: We are the world's only Bible. They may never read the Book, but they will read you. We are not all "apostles." But we are all "epistles of Christ known and read of all men."

2. Sin Is Sin!

   a) Unmentionable human acts (v. 3).

      1) "Fornication," Gr: PORNEIA, Sexual immorality! Involves all illicit sexual activity. Not just a premarital sex act.

      2) "Uncleanness," Impurity! Includes sexual sins first named, but probably includes all defiling practices such as prostitution and homosexuality.

      3) "Covetousness," Greed! Greedy, eager desire to have more, especially what belongs to others. Like Fornication: uncontrolled appetite.

      4) "Not once named," Gr: MEDE, "Not to speak of doing such a thing, let it not be even so much as mentioned among you."

   b) Inconvenient human talk (v. 4)

      1) "Filthiness," Obscenity! Shameless immoral conduct or talk.

      2) "Foolish talk," combine "moron" and "logos," to talk like a fool morally, godless, impure.

      3) "Jesting," Coarse Joking! Related closely to obscenity and immoral talk, but the emphasis is on the kind of coarse, vulgar wit, the lowest kind of humor.

   c) Two indications of character:

1) What makes you laugh or weep.

2) ILL: A Christian woman attended an anniversary dinner in honor of a friend. A program of low comedy followed the meal. The comedian tried to entertain the crowd with coarse humor that degraded everything the Christian held sacred and honorable. At a point in his program, the comedian's throat became dry. "Please bring me a glass of water," he asked. At that point the Christian woman added, "And bring a toothbrush and a bar of soap with it!" Certainly soap would never cleanse the conversation, but she made her point.

3) [Not] "Convenient," Gr: unseemly, unbefitting. Inappropriate. Improper. Does not pertain to. Does not fit.

B. Contrasts the Unmistakable Alternative (v. 4b)

Here is the contrasting positive side of this. It shows what a Christian is to be and do by contrast. I am sure v. 9 is one positive alternative referred to here. Yet there is another way of putting the proper Christian behavior in these areas. From the contrast Paul makes when he says, "Instead of immorality, impurity, immoral talk, and coarse joking, which are out of place for Christians," there should be "rather giving of thanks." But in contrast, what Paul has in mind is thanksgiving for the things which the vices distort and destroy. But when properly used they are great forces for good to all mankind.

1. The First of These Blessings is PROPER SEX, of which both immorality and impurity (v. 3) are the distortions!

   a) Sex is viewed from a negative point because pagan society has vulgarized it so much. We are to deplore and condemn only the distortions which destroy the good God intended.

   b) It is a God-given gift for man's good and is something for which we should give thanks. In it we seek to honor and please Him.

2. The Second of These Blessings for which we are to give thanks is our share of the world's MATERIAL POSSESSIONS!

a) When material possessions are distorted, thanksgiving turns into greed. Covetousness. Avarice. Inordinate desire for more. Always wants to have more. Never satisfied with what we have.

b) Things (money) are not bad within themselves. It is the love of things (money) that distorts and destroys the truth of God and defiles the heart of man.

c) Thankfulness is being content with what we have been given and accepting responsibility for using it properly for good.

3. The Third of These Blessings for which we are to give thanks is the REAL TRUTH and the ability to express it properly by words.

   a) Of which obscene language, impure talk, and coarse joking. But remember a bright spirit, a good sense of humor is not bad.

   b) ILL: The God who made monkeys is not without humor. If you want to see God's sense of humor, look at some of us.

   c) It is the distortion that defiles and destroys God's best for man.

C. **Warns of Unavoidable Consequences! (vv. 5–6)**

Here are some practical warnings of the unavoidable consequences of violation of these moral laws. The option is yours. You can violate them. But be warned of the unavoidable consequences.

1. The First Warning is That of Kingdom Exclusion! (v. 5)

   a) "Ye know" Gr: OIPA you know of a surety beyond a shadow of a doubt. It is a self-evident truth, knowledge.

   b) This is not excommunication from a church organization. It is exclusion from the Kingdom of God both here and hereafter.

2. The Second Warning is That of Empty Deceit! (v. 6a)

   a) These sins are proven to be mere shadows of empty deceit.

   b) They promise something they cannot deliver! Happiness! Joy! Good! Love!

  c) Sin and disobedience are deceivers! Don't let sin deceive you. Sinners! Commercials! Peers! Friends! Feelings! Your flesh! The pursuit of such things is vain, empty, hollow deceit.

3. The Third Warning is That of Divine Wrath! (v. 6b)

  a) These sins will incur the eternal wrath of the Almighty God! The violation makes you a child of disobedience.

   1) God hates sin. It incurs His hottest wrath. Behold the goodness and severity of the Lord.

   2) Sin will deprive you of Heaven and send you to hell. (See Rev. 22:14–15.)

  b) The unmentionable: Sexual immorality, Moral impurity! Greedy avarice! Shameless obscenity! Impure talk! Coarse joking!

   1) These sins incur the wrath of God because they involve a total disregard for divine law.

   2) These sins incur the wrath of God because they involve the utter perversion of human nature.

   3) These sins incur the wrath of God because they involve an all-out promotion of human misery in the universe.

CONCL: This passage closes with an imperative statement (v. 7).

A forbidden partnership! Watch yourself. No participation with them. Wicked enticers such as humanism speak empty hollow words: "It is pleasant and safe to do these things."

The truth is that such things make you children of disobedience. They will suffer the wrath of God. They bear the penalty of exclusion from Heaven.

Do not partake with them! Don't join them! Don't participate with them! Don't be partners with them!

ILL: In a place of business, an association ad read, "Partners In Excellence." But we can be partners in crime. And partners in sin. (See 1 Pet. 4:4.)

III.   WALKING IN LIGHT

Ephesians 5:8–14

INTRO: This chapter began with what believers called "followers ['imitators'] of God, as dear children" (v. 1). Walking in love, we are to imitate God's forgiving, giving, living love. A living love which avoids the unmentionable deeds of godless society and pursues the unmistakable alternative lifestyle, "as becometh saints" (v. 3). In these verses before us we are to imitate God by walking in light, "as children of light" (v. 8). The most important thing about this statement is that it does not say merely that before conversion we were "IN" darkness; and that now since conversion we are "IN" the light. Although that is true!

What is said is far more profound! Before conversion we "WERE" darkness! Now we "ARE" light! It points to the change in us, not just to the change in our surroundings.

Before we were not only in darkness, darkness was in us. And now we are not only in light, we are light. Therefore, we shine out as lights in this dark world.

It is not seeking the light, finding the light, or living in the light, it is being the light in darkness.

So becoming a Christian involves a change from darkness to light. And being a Christian involves shining in the darkness.

Life in sin is darkness! Life in Christ is light! God's Word says: "Called out of darkness into His marvelous light, children of light, children of the day, put on the armor of light—hold forth the Word of light—we shine as lights in the world."

ILL: Lighthouses do not ring bells and sound sirens to call attention to their light—they just shine.

He—Paul—points out some important things about walking in light:

A. Light Produces Good Fruit! (v. 9)

Better TR. "the fruit of the light." It is referring to the spiritual results of the light. The use of the word "all" means inclusive. All morality lies in these three virtues: the good, the right, and the true. These are not humanly achieved, but fruit of light.

1. The First Characteristic Light Produces is Goodness!

    a) In NT several Gr. words trans. "good—goodness."

        1) One of them means "intrinsically right, free from defects, beautiful, honorable."
        2) ILL: Used of God's creation, "everything created by God is good."

    b) Another means that which is "pleasant, useful, suitable, worthy." ILL: Used to declare, "Bad company corrupts good morals."

        1) But the one used here, GR: AGATHOSUNE refers to "moral excellence, to being good in both nature and effectiveness."
        2) A goodness that finds its fullest expression in that which is willingly and sacrificially done for others.
        3) This goodness primarily pertains to our relationship to others!

2. The Second Characteristic Light Produces is Righteousness!

    a) This virtue has first to do with our relationship with God.
    b) We are right with God. We are justified by God.
    c) But righteousness also has to do with how we live.
    d) Those who are made righteous are commanded to live righteously.
    e) See Rom. 6:13.

3. The Third Characteristic Light Produces is Truth!

    a) This "truth" has to do with honesty, reliability, trustworthiness, and integrity. It means being true. In contrast to the hypocritical, deceptive, and false ways of the old life of darkness.

    b) This relates primarily to oneself. Personal integrity. We are true, genuine, and real.

B. Light Proves Good Conduct! (vv. 8b, 10)

  1. Light Enables us to Discriminate/Determine What is Right!

    a) And what is wrong. In darkness there is no choice. It is the light that enables us to see the difference between things.

    b) ILL: In some small countries the stores/shops are just simple enclosures with no windows to let in light of day. Like a man about to buy a piece of silk cloth. Before he decides, he takes it out into the street and holds it up to the sun so that it reveals any hidden flaws in it.

      1) We are to prove every action, decision, and motive by the light. Hold it up to the Sun of Righteousness.

      2) Test every proposed course of action against the known will of God. (See Rom. 12:2.)

  2. Light Proves Our Life to be Truly Right!

    a) ILL: Before you board an airplane, your personal baggage must be checked by x-ray and sometimes hand-searched. Because they are not carrying weapons, hand grenades, explosives, or other illegal items, most people have no fear of sending their luggage through an x-ray machine. Because they have nothing to hide.

    b) Likewise, a Christian is not afraid to be scrutinized under the light of God's Word or even under the critical eye of a world looking for defects.

      1) We have nothing to hide.

      2) They will find nothing but the good, the right, and the true since we have come to the light.

C. Light Exposes Evil Deeds! (vv. 11–13)

Light and darkness just cannot mix or mingle. Not even in the physical world. Light reveals what darkness conceals. The light of day expels the darkness of night. Here are four Scriptural ways to expose evil:

1. Expose Evil by Refusing to Participate! (v. 11)
2. Expose evil by the light of a righteous life! We are not to be involved in evil even by association.

   a) ILL: We cannot witness to the world if we do not go out into the world. We cannot go far into the world before coming into contact with all sorts of wickedness.

   b) We are never to identify with such evil, nor give it opportunity to take hold in our life.

      1) ILL: The blessed man in Psalm 1 illustrates this truth!
      2) He "walketh not in the counsel of the ungodly."
      3) He "standeth not in the way of sinners."
      4) He "sitteth not in the seat of the scornful."
      5) This is a progression of evil: walk, stand, sit (Ps. 1:1)!
      6) We are not even to keep company with professed believers who are openly sinning. Paul's command is direct and simple.

   c) Children of light are to have nothing to do with the "unfruitful works of darkness."

      1) "Unfruitful" because darkness produces results in life, but not the kind one would wish to harvest.
      2) Unspecified "works of darkness" are typified by the specific sins already mentioned in chs. 4 and 5, such as deceit, falsehood, stealing, unwholesome speech, bitterness, wrath, anger, clamor, slander, malice, immorality, impurity, greed, filthiness, impure talk, coarse joking, covetousness, and idolatry.
      3) They bring no good to man, and no glory to God.

3. Expose Evil by Speaking as a Witness! (vv. 11b–12) Our responsibility goes farther than not participating in sinful deeds.

   a) But also, "rather reprove them" (v. 11).

   b) This statement can be so easily misunderstood and misapplied.

      1) It does not simply mean to reprimand, to condemn, to denounce. This is a hateful, hating, negative attitude. It was the Pharisaic attitude.

      2) It does not simply mean "preaching at" or applying moral standards to the problem.

      3) "Reprove" Gr: "to convince by means of evidence."

      4) It means by word of mouth and way of life to give enlightenment and understanding.

      5) "Them" refers to the sinful deeds, not to man!

   c) It means we are to throw light upon these things in such a manner that we really convince the person doing them of the harmful nature of what he is doing and what it means to his immortal, eternal soul.

   d) The best way to rid the world of any evil is to drag it out into the light. In the light, it dies a natural death.

   e) To rightly "reprove" means to throw the light of the gospel upon a man and his situation. By our ways. By God's Word.

      1) Sometimes open rebuke is necessary!

      2) TR: "set your face against them," that is, the sinful deeds. Expose them. Correct them. A Christian cannot confront sin with indifference. Sin must be met with intolerance.

      3) Failure to speak out against, to oppose evil is a failure to obey God.

      4) Some things are so shameful and disgraceful they should even be barred from conversation. Much more our lives.

4. Expose Evil by Shining God's Word! (v. 13)

    a) LIT: "All things become visible when they are exposed to the light." The light is God's Word, "for it is light that makes everything visible" (AMP).

    b) Light makes things manifest (visible). It shows them to be what they actually are. Revealed sin is seen for the ugliness it really is. Light dispels darkness. Whatever light falls on is no longer darkness, but belongs to light.

    c) Our resource for exposing sin is Scripture, The Light of the Word! (See Ps. 119:105, 130; Prov. 6:23; Heb. 4:12–13; 2 Tim. 3:16.)

CONCL: This passage closes with a poetic quotation (v. 14)! Paul uses it as though all his readers should know it. But today no one knows where it comes from. But almost certainly it was a fragment of an early church hymn. A compilation of several Psalms. It most probably was sung at the baptism of each church convert. The thought is that of a change from darkness to light. The message: Awake—Arise—Alive!

ILL: A group of tourists were visiting Carlsbad Caverns in New Mexico. Among those observing the wonders of this phenomenal underground cavern were a girl of 12 years and her 7-year-old brother. When they had reached the deepest part of the caverns, as was customary, the guide turned off the lights for a moment's meditation and silence. The little boy became frightened and began to cry. And there in the pitch-black darkness and quietness of this cave, many an adult received a moral lift from the clear whisper of the girl to her little brother. "Don't cry. Don't be afraid. There's someone here who knows where the lights are, and he can turn them on."

ILL: AFTER THE LAST LAMP IS DAWN!

The story is told of a man whose youth and early manhood had been spent in evil ways and who had been genuinely converted. He was one night sharing his testimony. He told of meeting an old drinking buddy during the week who in a good-natured way ridiculed him for becoming a Christian.

Christian, "I'll tell you what, you know what I am [he was the village lamplighter]; when I go round turning out the lights, I look back, and all the road over which I've been walking is all darkness, and that's what my past is like. I look on in front, and there's a long row of shining lights to guide me, and that's what the future is since I turned to Christ."

Drinking friend, "Yes, but by and by you get to the last lamp, and turn it out, and where are you then?"

Christian, "Then, why, when the last lamp goes out, it's dawn, and there ain't no need for lamps when the morning comes."

IV. WALKING IN WISDOM

Ephesians 5:15–20

INTRO: Godly wisdom is the first priority in living!

In my beginning as a pastor, my greatest concern was with acquiring facts and achieving skills necessary for an effective ministry. That is probably true of anyone entering a new field of work. However, as I grew older and matured some and gained some experience, I found myself looking for something else far more important than mere facts, knowledge, intelligence, and ability. I earnestly sought wisdom to apply these things: The common sense to translate facts, knowledge, and intelligence into ordinary, practical, everyday situations. Today I pray more for wisdom than anything else.

This is the emphasis of God's Word!

In the OT book of Proverbs, one third of its content pictures Wisdom standing in the streets, crying out for the wise and godly person to pursue her. She cries, "The fear of the Lord is the beginning of wisdom, And the knowledge of the Holy One is understanding" (9:10 NKJV).

In the NT Paul sets the record straight. He deplores the wisdom of the world and extols the wisdom of God. (See 1 Cor. 1:21–25.)

Knowledge of the truth of the gospel. The wisdom to apply it to the Christian life effectively. These are the two parts of this wisdom. First, its content is centered in the knowledge of Jesus Christ, the gospel. Second, the practical application of that knowledge to real-life experiences and situations. It is the second part of Wisdom with which this passage deals. There are three specific areas named here in which the believer is to exercise wisdom.

A. Wisdom in Making the Most of Time! (vv. 15–16)

Two ways we can wisely make the most of our life:

1. We Are to "Walk Circumspectly!" (v. 15)

   a) It speaks of conduct! "Walk" is a characteristic NT word referring to the whole of our conduct, behavior, and demeanor. The entirety of one's activity and manner. The whole of one's life among people. That is our walk.

   b) There is a connection! "Then" is a connective word which attaches walking wisely with the previous thought of light. We are children of light. We are light. So then walk wisely.

   c) There is a command! "See then" is an exhortation to take heed, beware, be careful. This walk is a matter of tremendous importance. Give it your personal attention.

   d) There is a contrast! "Not as fools, but as wise" is a contrast between the life of the Christian and the non-Christian. One is wise. The other is foolish. Common illustration: the two houses (see Matt. 7:24–27), the ten virgins (see Matt. 25: 1–13).

   e) There is a caution! "Walk circumspectly" Gr: "walk exactly, with strictness, on one's guard, carefully one step at a time." Our Eng. word means "looking all around." Like one walking in a dangerous place. It is a careful, cautious "walk" through this world of pollution and pitfalls.

   f) ILL: Like a man who walks on a beam of an unfinished building or on the edge of a roof, where just one misstep could mean a fatal fall.

2. We Are to Redeem Time! (v. 16)

   a) Making the most of our life. Buying up opportunities for ourselves. Right use of our time.

   b) Two things about our spot in history!

      1) We do not consider time as important as it is.

      2) Time is the stuff life is made up of.

   c) There are two things we have going for us in our calling to serve God: space and time. They are the "warp and woof," shape and content of history. Because they fix us at a particular point in God's vast plan of redemption. Space fixes us in a particular location! Such as America, state, city, or neighborhood. What we are going to do for God we must do here.

d) Time fixes us in a peculiar period of history. We are not in the 17th or 18th century of great revivals and missionary movements. We are in the 21st century. Our problems and opportunities are unique. The wise person recognizes this and acts accordingly.

e) The NT usage of the word "time." Gr: HEMERA, "day." HORA, "hour." KAIROS, "season." CHRONOS, "time." AION, "age." All of these have a unique association. Interestingly, the one used here is KAIROS "season." Better understood by contrasting it with CHRONOS "time." Chronos refers to the flow of time, the following of one event after another. The idea is our chronology.

f) KAIROS "season" refers to a moment that is especially significant or favorable. An opportune moment.

g) Paul is saying, there is a real conflict going on between good and evil. The days are evil. Therefore, seize every opportune moment to make a contribution for good.

B. Wisdom in Understanding the Will of the Lord! (v. 17)

The thought of redeeming time leads directly to understanding what the will of the Lord is.

1. The will of the Lord is not some mystical experience or special revelation. The general will of God can be found and studied in the Word of God.

2. But in this passage, I believe more than just knowing God's will as revealed in the Scripture. It speaks more of application of wisdom than of acquisition of facts.

a) It speaks particularly of what God is doing in history and our part in it.

b) Paul is talking about wisdom and about making the most of that specific historical time God gives us. The big questions are: What is God doing now? What are we to do with our moments, our life? What does God want us to be doing at this moment?

3. ILL: I am a little skeptical of programs, movements, and groups that promise to do something or other for God. Wisdom consists in perceiving where God is going and then getting going in that direction. Find out which way the Holy Spirit is flowing, and go with the flow.

    a) ILL: The unwise fool is being led astray into one "promising" program after another, attempting to do something for God, and so dissipates both time and energy.
    b) The wise person weighs these promising groups and strives to set a course through them in the direction he perceives God to be leading.

4. This wisdom is necessary for church leadership. There are so many programs available: growth, renewal, evangelism.
5. It takes divine wisdom to perceive God's direction for a particular church and follow it without deviation.

C. Wisdom of Being Filled with the Spirit! (vv. 18–20)

This is not speaking of the initial filling, but of a continual fullness of the Spirit. The Spirit-filled life.

1. In Acts there are at least nine other occasions after Pentecost when an individual or group of individuals is said to have been "filled with the Spirit."
2. The essence of spirituality is being "filled with the Spirit." So full there is no room for anything else.
3. Given here are three sure evidences of true spirituality:

    a) A Singing Heart! (v. 19)
    b) A Thankful Heart! (v. 20)
    c) A Submissive Heart! (v. 21)

4. The influence of a Spirit-filled life spills over into all of life's relationships.

CONCL: "Singing and making melody in your heart" (v. 19).

Not everyone can make "melody" on an instrument. It can be noise. "Melody" depends on the condition of the instrument and the skill of the player. Every believer's heart is like a harp; as the Holy Spirit breathes upon the heartstrings, real melody goes up to the ear of God. The joy of the Holy Ghost that filled NT Christian hearts is upward on wings of song. Their very talk was music. Their souls were full of love. Their mouths were full of praise. They knew WHOM they praised and WHY they praised Him. There was no trace of sourness and bitterness. The whole Bible thrills with holy song. Even dungeons ring with it when they are there. The Christian sings for gladness of heart. Though tears may fill my eyes, the Lord's song fills my mouth because joy fills my heart. We cannot always be engaged in singing, but we can always maintain the spirit of song.

Walking in wisdom! We are to make the most of our time in the history of time and grab every opportune moment to serve God and contribute to good. We are to understand what God is doing in our period of history and our part in it. We are to be so filled with the Spirit that we reflect a singing, thankful, submissive heart at all times. (See vv. 15–21.)

V. WALKING IN HARMONY

Ephesians 5:21

INTRO: Living in Harmony is God's purpose for all created order! The universe! The world! In society! In the church! In the family! However, harmonious relationships require mutual submission. Hence the injunction, "Submitting yourselves one to another in the fear of God."

Striking statement! Misunderstood subject! Mutual submission! This is not an independent exhortation. Because it begins with a continuing word, "submitting." It is more than an introduction to what is to follow. It is actually a continuation of what was said before. Paul had just given the command, "be filled with the Spirit" (v. 18). Followed by three evidences of the Spirit-filled life: a singing heart (v. 19), a thankful heart (v. 20), and a submissive heart (v. 21).

Then proceeds to offer three examples of submission: the submission of wives to husbands (v. 22), the submission of children to parents (6:1–3), and the submission of slaves to masters (6:5–8). That is not to say that submission is the same in each case. Each of these relationships is unique. Yet they all have one thing in common. Each involves submission.

No one can practice the submission this verse teaches unless they are "filled with the Spirit" (v. 18). Submission is a product of the Holy Spirit. The world not only does not do it. They will not do it. They cannot do it.

If we are to submit ourselves "one to another," we must be different from those who are "filled with wine" (v. 18) and go to that excess. We must be "filled with the Spirit." Unlike what we were before. Unlike what the world is now.

This verse contains the two essentials to practicing mutual submission, which allows us to live in harmony.

A. Reverence for Our Father God! (v. 21b)

1. "In the fear of God." Fear means in awe of, in reverence to God.

2. In Reverence For Divine Order!

    a) The Bible contains a clear doctrine of Christian submission.

    b) Contained in the principle of authority and submission and the principle of mutual submission.

    c) The principle of authority and submission was instituted by God for the purpose of structure and function.

    d) All are equal in God's sight. (See Gal. 3:28.) But the principle of authority and submission was instituted by God for the purpose of order in structure and function.

        1) In secular society (the world, government). (See Rom. 13:1; 1 Pet. 2:13–14.)

        2) In the church. (See 1 Thess. 5:12–13; 1 Tim. 5:17; 1 Cor. 16:15–16; 1 Pet. 5:5; Heb. 13:17.)

        3) In the family. (See vv. 22–24; 6:1–3; Col. 3:18, 20, 22.)

3. In Reverence For Social Good!

    a) Submission is a matter of attitude! Obedience is a matter of conduct! What is the measure of obeying delegated authority? When delegated authority (men who represent God's authority) and direct authority (that is, God Himself) are in conflict, a believer must render submission but not obedience.

    b) Let me explain:

    c) Obedience is related to conduct and is relative.

    d) Submission is related to attitude and is absolute.

    e) God alone receives unqualified obedience without measure. Any power-position-person below God can receive only qualified obedience.

    f) Should delegated authority require or request something which clearly contradicts direct authority of God's Word, he should be given submission but not obedience.

    g) We should submit to the power-position-person of delegated authority from God but must disregard any order which offends God's direct authority.

B. Respect for Our Fellow Christians! (v. 21a)

1. "Submitting yourselves one to another." This is the principle of mutual submission in the Body of Christ.

2. It is a Voluntary Submission!

   a) "Submitting" Gr: HUPOTASSO, originally a military term meaning to arrange, line up, get in order, or rank under.

   b) As Christians we are to rank ourselves under one another. The whole mentality of the Christian life as we relate to each other is one of humility and submission.

   c) "Submitting yourselves." That is individual and voluntary. It cannot be forced. Even God will not do it for you. It is your personal, voluntary, volitionary commitment.

3. It is a Mutual Submission! "One to another."

   a) In terms of structure and function, there is to be authority and submission.

   b) In terms of interpersonal relationships, there is to be mutual submission. The principle of authority and submission is in the government, the church, and the home. But that does not change the fact that believers are to mutually submit to each other.

   c) It is this mutual submission called for here in these three examples:

      1) Wives are to submit to their husbands (v. 22), but (v. 25) husbands are to also submit to their wives. Question, "In what way?" There is no greater act of submission than to die for somebody. Husbands are to submit to their wives, not in the sense of abdicating their responsibility of leadership (headship), but in the sense of getting under her to bear her burdens, to carry her cares, to meet her needs, and to sacrifice himself to fulfill her needs.

      2) Children are to submit in obedience to their parents (6:1–3), but (6:4) the parents are to submit to their children. Submit in the sense that they are not to provoke them

to wrath, but instead "bring them up in the nurture and admonition of the Lord."

3) A servant is to submit to his master (6:5–8), but (6:9) a master submits to never doing to that servant beyond what is right.

d) We are all to submit somewhere. All of these relationships illustrate mutual submission. Paul is speaking to the whole church, "submitting yourselves one to another in the fear of God."

CONCL: This verse calls for a submission to one another based on reverence for God. When we really reverence, fear, stand in awe of, and worship God, we will be submitting to one another. This is so vital to the church. Quarrels and conflicts in the church and the family come from the lust to be great and dominant. The exact opposite to submission. (See 1 Pet. 5:5.) One evidence of spirituality, being filled with the Spirit, is that of submission. The lusts of pride and arrogance wish to dominate, rule. The power of the Spirit leads one to mutual submission. So in reverence to God's Divine Order for social good, and in respect for our fellow believers, we happily submit to one another.

The filling of the Spirit prompts: wives to submit to their husbands; husbands to submit to wives; children to submit to parents; parents to submit to children; servants to submit to masters; and masters to submit to servants. This sets the stage for walking in harmony in all the relationships of life. I read a story that illustrates submission perfectly!

ILL: During the Great Reformation, two of the leading reformers became embittered in controversy. One of them, while walking in the mountains of Switzerland, was confronted with a soul-stirring sight.

He saw two goats making their way over a narrow path on the mountain. One was ascending the trail, the other descending. They were forced to pass at a point where the trail was so narrow that there was room for only one goat. He watched to see what happened. The animals rounded a turn in the path, which brought them in sight of each other. They backed up, as though ready to lunge in conflict, and then an amazing thing happened.

The goat on the trail below lay down in the path, while the goat above him walked over his back. The first animal then arose and continued his journey up the trail.

In Christ, the way down is the way up. Christ humbled Himself so that man could walk over Him into the Kingdom of Light, knowing afterward He would be exalted.

VI. HARMONY IN MARRIAGE

Ephesians 5:22–33

INTRO: Four-year-old Suzie had just heard the story of Snow White for the first time in her life. She could hardly wait to get home from nursery school to tell her mommy. With wide-eyed excitement, she related the fairy tale to her mother that afternoon. After relating how Prince Charming had arrived and kissed Snow White back to life, Suzie loudly asked, "And do you know what happened then?" Her mom said, "Yes, they lived happily ever after." Then Suzie replied with a frown, "No, they didn't; they got married." It is a glaring truth. Getting married and living happily ever after are not necessarily one and the same.

The national stats give us a grim graph of a growing divorce rate. In 1960, there were 25 divorces in every 100 marriages in America. In 1975, the rate had jumped to 48 divorces in 100 marriages. By 1990, the rate was about 60 divorces in every 100 marriages.

There is nothing in this world better than a good marriage. Conversely, there is nothing worse than a bad marriage. The major problem is that couples have departed from God's original design. The Divine blueprint has been either changed or ignored altogether.

As we enter this section of Scripture on marriage, a proverbial sign hangs at the door: DISASTER AREA; ENTER AT YOUR OWN RISK! Why? The American family is in trouble. Bad trouble. Marriages are hurting. Even Christian marriages. Strangely enough, the happily married couple seems an oddity in our time. So sad, yet so true!

The holy marriage state has always been a target of satanic attack.

Consider the conditions of marriage in Bible times.

The JEWS treated women like servants and divorced their wives for any frivolous reason they chose.

The GREEKS, even worse, treated wives as legitimate childbearers and managers of the household, who could be divorced without even legal proceedings. Men openly practiced fornication and prostitution. Society was dominated by homosexuality, lesbianism, and sexual abuse of children.

The ROMANS stooped lowest by reducing marriage to legalized prostitution because divorce was so easy. Children were unwanted because they cramped the woman's lifestyle and hurt the looks of her body. Women wanted to do everything that men did: wrestlers, fencers, hunters.

This was the condition of marriage when Paul wrote, "Wives, submit yourselves unto your own husbands, as unto the Lord. . . . Husbands, love your wives, even as Christ loved the church" (vv. 22, 25). This was not a reminder of what they already knew. He was calling them to a new standard of living. To them it was a divesting, dynamic, different lifestyle. There are two words here that describe harmony in marriage: submission and love. In Paul's injunction to wives and husbands, he declares a basic role of each and then gives an analogy to illustrate the significance of that role.

A. The Submission of a True Wife! (vv. 22–24)

The responsibility (role) of the wife in the marriage relationship is submission to her husband. The analogy is "as unto the Lord" (v. 22).

These verses contain the Divine key to any woman's being a happy, fulfilled, and successful wife.

1. This Submission Involves No Loss of Self Respect or Dignity! (v. 22)

   a) "Submit" same Gr. word used in v. 21 referring to Christian submission to one another.

   b) "Submit" Gr: "placing yourselves beneath." Speaks of a voluntary act by her choice. Not less than, nor inferior to. Someone can be "over" you in role, and yet not "above" you as a person.

   c) It also denotes fidelity when it says, "your own husband." If you have a compliment, a smile, a kind word, give it to your own husband.

    d) It does not say, "Wives, obey your husbands." "Submit" is a very mild and loving word.

2. This Submission is Defined by Spiritual Obligation!

    a) "As unto the Lord" (v. 22).

    b) It means to respond to your own husband as unto the Lord.

        1) The way one responds to the Lord is that we love Him because He first loved us. "Your own husband" makes it a very personal and loving relationship as the basis for submission.

        2) We also submit to the Lord voluntarily. Not forced submission, obedience, or subjection.

    c) This further emphasizes lack of inferiority. Before God there is "neither male nor female" (Gal. 3:28). Husband and wife are equal before God, and each is separately responsible to Him. God has first claim upon each of them. The submission commanded here is not a subjection of an inferior to a superior. It is a voluntary, personal, sympathetic submission that can only be rendered by an equal to an equal.

3. This Submission Recognizes the Husband's Leadership! (vv. 23–24)

    a) "The husband is the head of the wife." That phrase is often quoted in isolation. And that leads to misplaced emphasis on subordination. But the basis of this passage is not control, but love. It is qualified with "even as Christ is the head of the church." It is complemented with "and he is the saviour of the body." The pattern of this relationship is love. In that submission, there is liberty, not slavery.

    b) ILL: The first woman usurped the place of the man when she disobeyed God and took the forbidden fruit. Because of her leading the way in sin, as a part of the curse, she was subjected to the domination of her husband. (See Gen. 3:16.)

B. The Love of a Good Husband! (vv. 25–33)

The responsibility (role) of the husband in the marriage relationship is adoration of his wife. The analogy is "even as Christ also loved the church." The husband's love is the basis of the wife's submission. This prevents submission from ever becoming degrading as subjection to a tyrant must be. See v. 25 NIV. Most men's first response: "Impossible. I'm only human. Christ is Divine." Impossible as it sounds, it can be done for two reasons: God never told anyone to do something He was incapable of doing. God has made provision for us to love each other through the power of His Spirit. Here we have the Bible formula to being a good husband:

1. This Love Gives Sacrificially For Her Welfare! (v. 25)

   a) Sacrificial love. Never selfish. Never "Me first."

   b) He puts the welfare of his wife above his own: Ready to make any sacrifice for her good.

   c) A husband must come to terms with his role and answer the penetrating question, "Do I love my wife enough to die for her?"

   d) ILL: Matthew Henry used this analogy: "God didn't take a bone from the foot of Adam so he could trample his wife underfoot. He didn't take a bone from his head so that his wife could rule over him. Instead, God took a rib from the side of Adam, from close to his heart, so that man would love his wife, protect her, and keep her by his side."

2. This Love Elevates Her and Promotes Her Highest Interest (vv. 26–27).

   a) He wanted her cleansed, sanctified, glorious, and holy without spot, wrinkle, blemish, or any such thing.

   b) It is a purifying love. If it drags a person down, it's not love. The woman's worth is ENHANCED and her life is ENRICHED by a husband who adores her. There is in that context fulfillment and freedom seldom experienced elsewhere on earth.

3. This Love Cares Sincerely For Her Feelings and Comfort!

    a) Sometimes in the blind rush of life and familiarity of relationships, men forget how fragile marriage and wife are. "FRAGILE, HANDLE WITH CARE." Gentleness. Kindness. Courtesy. Wives should be cherished (vv. 28–32). This care is based on the sacredness of the marriage bond, "they two shall be one flesh" (v. 31).

    b) This bond makes it an unbreakable relationship. Separation would mean to tear yourself apart. She is your "help meet," your counterpart. You are made complete by her.

CONCL: Tucked away in these verses are two implied yet penetrating questions each partner must answer. The wife must come to terms of submission with her role and ask, "Do I love my husband enough to LIVE for him?" The husband must come to grips with his role of adoration and ask, "Do I love my wife enough to DIE for her?" (v. 33) "Nevertheless" brings us back down to earth with a jolt of reality. This is the practical part about marriage. How sin has marred this glorious relationship like everything else. The battle of the sexes is on. The woman fights to control the man. The man fights to subdue her. That's the curse of sin.

But the curse of sin is cured in Jesus Christ. When people love the Lord and are filled with the Spirit, wives submit, husbands love. And we are right back the way it was before the fall with Adam and Eve. They were co-regents. It was beautiful. They multiplied together. Filled the earth together. Subdued the earth together. Ruled together. That's God's ordained, created plan, pure and pristine for man and woman.

ADDITIONAL NOTES: Harmony In Marriage!

ILL: "Husbands, love your wives."

I read the story of a schoolboy who did a paper on Benjamin Franklin. He did his research and then squirmed into his chair, chewed his pencil, took a piece of paper, wrote at the top of it "Benjamin Franklin," and produced the following masterpiece:

"Benjamin Franklin was born in Boston, but he soon got tired of that and moved to Philadelphia. When he got to Philadelphia, he was hungry, so he bought a loaf of bread. He put the bread under his arm. He walked up the street; he passed a woman. The woman smiled at him. He married the woman and discovered electricity."

Every man ought to marry a woman and discover electricity. That's what Paul had in mind when he wrote, "Husbands, love your wives."

Russian Proverb: "Before going to war, pray once; before going to sea, pray twice; before getting married, pray three times."

The greatest of all the arts is the art of living together.

CONCL: Women have been oppressed by the crushing power of men who want to keep them subdued. Men have been hassled by women who want to rise to the top and take over.

But Christians have the answer—Jesus Christ! When Christ lives in the heart and you are filled with the Spirit, all of a sudden, men and women submit to the God-ordained pattern, and the home becomes like it was in the Garden of Eden before the fall.

> TOGETHER they are fruitful!
> TOGETHER they multiply!
> TOGETHER they have dominion!
> TOGETHER they subdue!
> TOGETHER they work out the plan of God in their lives.

Christianity is not offering to the world a suppression of women and the exaltation of men, or vice versa. Christ offers the power of the Holy Spirit, by which men and women can fulfill their role and responsibilities toward each other as God ordained. When this happens, the home becomes a place where spiritual life functions, and the children are blessed after them.

ILL: The word "husband" comes from "house-band." Thus the husband is the one who binds the house together. LIT: "the band of the house; the support of the house; the one who keeps it together, as a band keeps together a sheaf of corn."

✤ Chapter 6 ✤

PRESERVATION: THE CHRISTIAN WALK

—HARMONY AND VICTORY

Ephesians 6:1–24

INTRO: This chapter brings to a conclusion the Christian walk. It closes with the believer walking in victory.

I.   HARMONY AT HOME (6:1–4)

    A.   The Fathers are Under Attack
    B.   The Mothers are Under Attack
    C.   The Children are Under Attack

II.   RESPECTFUL CHILDREN (6:1–3)

    A.   The Act of Obedience (v. 1)
    B.   The Attitude of Honor (vv. 2–3)

III.   FAITHFUL PARENTS (6:4)

    A.   Demonstrate the Quality of Gentleness (v. 4a)
    B.   Demonstrate the Standard of Godliness (v. 4b)

IV.   HARMONY AT WORK (6:5–9)

    A.   The Duty of Christian Employees (vv. 5–8)
    B.   The Duty of Christian Employers (v. 9)

V.   WALKING IN VICTORY (6:10–13)

    A. The Inspired Instructions of the Spirit (vv. 10–11a)

    B. The Invisible Enemy of the Church (vv. 11b–13)

VI. OUR REAL ENEMY (6:11–12)

    A. Satan is A Great and Powerful Foe

    B. Satan is A Wicked and Destructive Seducer

    C. Satan is A Sly and Crafty Deceiver

VII. WINNING THE VICTORY (6:14–17)

    A. We Must Know for Certain the Absolute Truth (v. 14a)

    B. We Must Make a Firm Commitment to Right Living (v. 14b)

    C. We Must Always Be Ready to Stand Up for the Gospel (v. 15)

    D. We Must Hold Fast to a Simple Trust in God (v. 16)

    E. We Must Know for Sure (We are Saved) (v. 17)

VIII. WEAPONS OF OUR WARFARE (6:18–24)

    A. The Word is Our Mighty Weapon (v. 17b)

    B. The Weapon of Prayer is Our Secret Resource (v. 18)

I. HARMONY AT HOME

Ephesians 6:1–4

INTRO: Now WALKING IN HARMONY moves to the parent-child relationship. Harmony in marriage and harmony at home are both illustrations of the Christian principle of mutual submission stated in 5:21. Like marriage, harmony at home in the parent-child relationship depends entirely on mutual submission.

If the family system breaks down, it will be the third in human history: first in ancient Greece and second in the Roman Empire. The family and home are under terrific pressure today!

ILL: The story is told of a realtor who contacted a newly married couple with the goal of selling them a home. After hearing the sales pitch, the young bride replied, "Who needs a home? I was born in a hospital, reared in a daycare nursery, lived in a suitcase, ate in a restaurant, and married in a church. Who needs a home? All we need is a garage for the compact car, and a bedroom above it in which to change our clothes and sleep."

Millions of homes are ending annually in divorce courts. Millions more are holding together in misery, unhappiness. Even the best of homes are plagued with instability, insecurity. Our nation's strength depends upon family life.

The home and family in America could be designated as a NATIONAL EMERGENCY, if we are to remain a nation.

The strength of the church depends upon the spiritual status of its families. An unhappy family member cannot be a productive member of the Body of Christ. Apathy and indifference there spill over into the church.

Look at our world and you can understand the importance of this text.

Satan is attacking the family. The situation is critical. The satanic attack on God's design for marriage has had a residual effect on the home in America. (Half of marriages end in divorce.)

We have moved away from the Divine plan that God established for the family and home. I want to show some of Satan's strategies employed against the family in America today.

A. The Fathers are Under Attack!

1. Many Have Abandoned Their God-Given Role.

   a) God has established the father as the head of the home, the leader of the family.

   b) ILL: One leading psychologist argues that if the man is not the head of the family, there can be nothing but chaos. He is responsible for structure and form; for establishing family standards, character, direction, and strength. If he does not, he puts the family in jeopardy.

2. Many Have Diverted From Their Responsibilities!

   a) Their attention has been diverted from their wives and children to fulfill their own desires. To become macho man. To be self-satisfied.

   b) They lose concentration on loving the family, providing for their family, caring for their family, and offering strength, stability, security, leadership, and teaching to their family. Preoccupied with the TV set, their businesses, making money, accumulating material things, or lust for other women and any other thing which diverts priorities.

3. Many Have Even Completely Deserted Their Family!

   a) Divorce is easy. Grass is greener. Wife and kids are left to fend for themselves. No regrets. No remorse.

   b) ILL: The modern TV portrait of the father is that he is a wimpy, weakly, ignorant sort of person of little importance to the family's well-being.

B. The Mothers are Under Attack!

1. She is Forced Out of the Home!

a) Reasons: no husband, family budget, desire for more things

b) ILL: Presently nearly one-half of the American workforce are women. More than 6 million children under 6 years have working mothers. One-half of all children under 18 years have working mothers.

2. She is Intimidated to Leave the Home!

a) They are told in college: "Don't let yourself settle into being a homemaker. You're too good for that. Push yourself out into the world."

b) In the work world, there are temptations: other men, material things, worldly philosophies, worldly lifestyles.

C. The Children are Under Attack!

1. Abandoned At Home!

a) "One major change in middle-class mothering. For a mother to work voluntarily while her children were young, was once seen as a sign of bad parenting, a rejection of her maternal role. But today, going to work and placing a child in a daycare center is accepted practice."[1]

b) For the children that means coming home to an empty house after school. Tending to their own hygiene, clothing, and meals. Many lock the doors on school holidays and sit in front of the TV all day long.

2. Influenced By TV

a) Violent role-models. We are raising a generation of violently aggressive men and women who are being formed through children's exposure to TV's fantasy, which is extremely violent.

b) Godless morality. Many writers are warning America. Interviews with the forces behind TV (e.g., prod. writers) reveal that they are systematically attempting to overthrow traditional American values. Much through comedy; if they

---

1   David Eklund, "Growing Up Faster," Psychology Today (Feb. 1979): 41.

can get people to laugh at something, they can gloss over the real issues, get them to buy it because it is funny.

   c) ILL: While children are watching TV, alcohol is being used ten-to-one to any other beverage. Most of all sex depicted on TV is outside marriage. Stifled communication with parents. Tragically, many parents don't talk to their children because they are too busy watching TV.

3.   Raised by Daycare Centers!

   a) In Denver, daycare workers were so frustrated, they were attempting to start a union to protect themselves from the abusive little brats that people keep dropping off.

   b) They come with runny noses, chicken pox, and bad manners. The daycare mother must teach them everything at a fifty-to-one ratio.

   c) ILL: Alarming American Children Statistics!

      1) In 1979, an estimated three-quarter million children lived in foster homes, residential facilities, institutions, mental hospitals, or were incarcerated in prisons.

      2) Four out of ten children will live in a broken home.

      3) Eighteen million children currently live with stepparents.

      4) Between 7 and 14 million will become alcoholics.

      5) They are indulged with over 4 billion dollars' worth of toys each year, more than the gross national product of 63 nations.

      6) The average age of beginning smokers has dropped from 14 to 10.

      7) One million young girls between the ages of 12 and 17 get pregnant every year.

      8) The only age of increased births in America is girls from ages 11 to 14.

      9) Ten million minors have VD, and 5,000 new victims get it every day—those are minors.

      10) One child in five uses drugs twice a week.

    d) Our children are under satanic attack. We can't stand around indifferent to the whole thing and expect they will turn out all right in the end.

CONCL: Children are being victimized by an emerging humanistic philosophy.

ILL: A well-known humanist author travels around the country and speaks in colleges about the future: "We must settle for nothing less than the total elimination of the family."[2] That is what is being propagated by humanists in our USA, and they are very effective.

ILL: The United Nations Declaration of the Rights of the Child seemed very innocent when first adopted in 1959. However, when you see how it has been defined today, it is a whole different story.

    1. Liberation from traditional morals and values! (Lessen parental influence.) Gloria Steinem, "By the year 2000 we will, I hope, raise our children to believe in human potential, not God."

    2. Liberation from parental authority! Free children from physical punishment, free them to vote, and give them sexual freedom. The goal: class-less, sex-less, God-less, family-less society.

    3. Liberation from any form of discrimination! "The child shall be protected from practices which may foster racial, religious, or any other form of discrimination." Children removed from any kind of religious teaching. They just grow up and decide for themselves.

    4. Liberation from nationalism and patriotism. It is usually the family who teaches such patriotism. The school must not teach such. Family must not teach love for the country.

I thank God for His precious Word. It tells us how to counter the godless plot to destroy our families and homes. The answer is twofold: Children obey, honor, and respect your parents. Submission! Parents bring your children up in the nurture and admonition of the Lord. Only that simple truth will bring harmony at home!

---

2   F. M. Esfandiary, *Up-Wingers: A Futurist Manifesto* (New York: John Day Co., 1973), 20.

ILL: The Bible gives a standard for the conduct of individual family members. The story is told that during the administration of confirmation to a class of girls about to enter the Catholic Church, a young girl was asked, "What is matrimony?" Making a face, she said, "Oh, matrimony is a state of terrible torment which those who enter are compelled to undergo for a time to fit them for heaven." The young priest said, "Oh, no, you have given the definition of purgatory. It is matrimony we are talking about." The Archbishop interrupted, "What do you know about it? Maybe she is right." Whether a home is purgatory or paradise depends upon the attitudes of the people within the home.

II. RESPECTFUL CHILDREN

Ephesians 6:1–3

INTRO: Remember, this section of Scripture is talking about living in harmony in all life's relationships. A harmony based on the principle of mutual submission. That submission is based on a reverence for God. Stated in 5:21, this mutual submission is one of the evidences of the indwelling Christ and the Spirit-filled life. These verses are addressed directly to "children." In them are the children's specific contributions (role or duty) to harmony at home in the parent-child relationship.

ILL: After watching a TV presentation about rebellious youth, a husband said to his wife, "What a mess! Where did our generation go wrong?" The wife calmly answered, "We had children." It is the perpetual children problem. Children and youth in every generation get a bad rap.

ILL: Try to date this opinion: "Children now love luxury, have bad manners, contempt for authority, show disrespect for their elders, and love chatter in place of exercise. Children are now tyrants, not the servants of households. They no longer rise when elders enter the room. They contradict their parents, chatter before company, gobble up their dainties at table, cross their legs, and tyrannize over their teachers." (Socrates, Greek Teacher, 400 BC)

Oh the generation gap! Much is said about how different youth are today than when we were young. In reality, there isn't much difference.

- They say they want to be understood! Just what I wanted.

- They say they can't talk to their parents! Neither could I about everything.

- They say they want reasons, not rules! My feelings exactly.

- They say they are more enlightened than their parents, and therefore are not on the same level! My thoughts precisely.

The problem with youth is youth! Parent-child problems, like history, repeat themselves with every generation. The real difference is respect and understanding. Respect from the youth. Understanding from the parents. It is this troublesome problem which every youth in every generation faces that Paul addresses here. There are two specific duties of "CHILDREN" in the parent-child relationship mentioned here:

A. The Act of Obedience! (v. 1)

1. The child who obeys without question is probably too young to talk!
2. Obedience is the child's first lesson and must be learned well.
3. ILL: Like the policeman who noticed a boy with a large pack of stuff on his back riding a tricycle around and around the block. Finally, he asked him where he was going. The child replied, "I'm running away from home." Policeman, "Then why do you keep going around and around the block?" Reply, "Well, my mother won't let me cross the street."
4. "Obey" Gr: two words, one means "to hear" and the other means "under." So the Holy Spirit is saying, "Children, get under the authority of your parents, and listen."
5. Two important things are said to children about obedience:

   a) Obedience Has Divine Sanction! "In the Lord."

      1) It is the Christian thing to do. The submission called for in 5:21 is Christian submission. Becoming a Christian reinforces our normal obligations of life. Christian faith makes a better child at home.
      2) Parallel verse: Col. 3:20.
      3) Remember direct authority and delegated authority. All of us owe obedience and respect to those over us, but not at the expense of the obedience we owe to God.
      4) ILL: In the great spiritual chapter John 15: the secret of abounding is abiding; the secret of abiding is obeying; and the secret to obeying is abandonment to Christ.

   b) Obedience Harmonizes With Natural Order! "For this is right."

1) It is the right thing to do! It is a law of conduct. It is the order of nature. It is God-ordained. That argues for the rightness of an action. Obedience is the law of the universe. Without it, everything would rush into chaos and destruction.

2) Obey! "This is right." Right is a law of conduct not based on custom or conviction; it arises from eternity and is seated deep in our nature. It is based on Biblical and eternal principles.

3) The world's standard for right action:

   a. This is customary. Power of tradition, opinion, fashion.

   b. This is profitable.

   c. This is popular.

   d. This is pleasant.

   e. This is clever.

4) God's standard: "This is right." The rule of right is the declared will of God.

B. The Attitude of Honor! (vv. 2–3)

Honor is the attitude behind the act of obedience.

1. If you get the attitude right, the act will follow. Wrong attitudes will always destroy good relationships.

2. "Honor" Gr: TIMAO, "to value highly, to hold in the highest regard and respect, even reverence." It means to show them respect and love, to care for them as long as they need you, and to seek to bring honor to them by the way you live.

3. This word is for children of all ages, for regardless of our age, we are all children of someone. Our behavior anywhere reflects on our parents. Honor is higher than obedience.

4. Honor parents:

   a) By treating them with respect at all times!

   b) By the way we talk TO and ABOUT them!

   c) By being patient with them as they grow older!

  d) By the way we live to the end of life!

  e) By caring for them in times of need and old age!

5. Two important truths about the attitude of honor:

  a) Honor of Parents Is Commanded by God! (v. 2)

   1) The first 4 of the Ten Commandments relate to God and do not have promises with them. The 5th commandment is the first relating to human relationships. (See Ex. 20:12; Deut. 5:16.)

   2) The 5th commandment is so important that God puts a promise with it. Important because it is the key to all human relationships and the passing on of a righteous heritage.

   3) ILL: This is God's way of making families that stick together. The parents raise the children; and when the children are grown, they take care of their parents. And while the grown children are taking care of their parents, they are raising their own children, who are going to take care of them while they are raising their children, and on and on it goes.

  b) Honor of Parents Is Blessed of God! (v. 3)

   1) This is the promise of God's blessings in life.

   2) It is a twofold promise:

    a. The quality of life, "that it may be well with thee." This promise of well-being refers to a full, rich life. Though its blessings may not always be tangible, a family where there is mutual love and respect will have a rich, God-given harmony and satisfaction that other families can never know.

    b. The quantity of life, "that thou mayest live long on the earth."

     i. The promise of longevity.

     ii. The believer who honors his parents can know that his lifetime will be the full measure God intends. It will not be cut short like Ananias and Sapphira.

    iii. Prosperity and longevity are the two most sought-for favors on earth.

CONCL: A parting word to parents: Honor and respect are always earned. No one is ever honored for what they receive; honor is always the reward of what one gives.

Every parent is proud of their children. They want the best for them. All parents want to be able to say: "I have respectful children. . . . I have Christian children."

The two strong character/behavioral traits of Christian children are obedience and honor! It is simple but sure! Practicing honor and obedience promises long life and well-being. Obedience and honor are the pathway to life and safety.

ILL: A railroad switchman was set to pull the lever for an oncoming train when, just at the critical moment, he turned his head and saw his little boy playing between the rails on which the train was running. He stuck to his lever and shouted to the child, "Lie down! Lie down!" The train passed and the father rushed over to pick up what he feared would be the mangled body of his child. But to his great joy, the boy had at once obeyed his order and lain down, and the train had passed over him without injury. This prompt obedience saved his life.

Here is God's Word directly addressed to "Children:" (1) "Obey your parents" (v. 1); (2) "Honour thy father and thy mother" (Ex. 20:12). It can be done in the power of the Spirit-filled life.

Interpersonal relationships are easy when one is "filled with the Spirit" (5:18). The husband-wife, master-servant, and parent-child. A happy wife must "be filled with the Spirit." A loving husband must "be filled with the Spirit."

If those who are older and much more experienced need to be filled with the Spirit to successfully fulfill their duty, how much less can children be expected to exemplify these godly traits without this glorious blessing. "Be filled with the Spirit."

III. FAITHFUL PARENTS

Ephesians 6:4

INTRO: Remember, this passage in Ephesians is talking about Living In Harmony in all life's relationships. This harmony is one of the evidences of the Spirit-filled life. It is based on mutual submission in 5:21. This mutual submission influences every relationship: marriage (husband-wife); family (parent-child); and vocation (master-servant).

This verse specifically focuses on parental responsibility to harmony at home in the parent-child relationship.

Raising children has never been easy. But it is always rewarding. It seems tougher now than ever.

ILL: A gentleman noticed a lady with ten children getting on the bus. He asked politely, "Are all these yours, or are you going on a picnic?" She replied, "They're all mine—and it's no picnic!" Sometimes family life is "no picnic." In tough times like these, it can be quite exasperating.

What a world to bring children into! Today's world does not even like children.

- There are one million unborn babies murdered by abortion every year in America alone!

- One-third of all married couples who are of childbearing age are permanently sterilized. They don't want children.

- One survey (1979) in America showed that 70% of the parents who responded would not have children if they had to do it over again.

- There is now an organization in the US called N.O.N. (The National Organization of Non-parents). Their stated purpose is not to foul up their lives with kids.

ILL: A school teacher remarked to her class that stats indicate more twins are being born now than ever before. One bright little third grader said, "I guess more twins are being born because little children are afraid to come into this world alone."

This command was given in times like ours. The children's status in Paul's time was deplorable.

- The Roman father had the right of PATRIA POTESTAS (The Father's Power). Under this law, he had absolute power over his family. He could sell them as slaves. He could make them work in his fields even in chains. He could take the law into his own hands and punish them any way he wished. He could inflict the death penalty on his child. Further, the power of the Roman father extended over the child's whole life, so long as the father lived. A Roman child never came of age. Even when he was grown he remained under his father's absolute power.

- It was the Roman father's right to decide whether or not his newborn child would live or die. When a child was born, it was placed before the father's feet. If the father stooped and lifted the child, that meant he wished it to live. If he turned and walked away, that meant he refused to acknowledge it. The child was quite literally thrown out.

- All children who were born weakly and deformed were drowned by order of the law. How pagan! How merciless! How unthinkable! Yet true!

It was to fathers who knew such practices that Paul dared to write. This verse specifically addresses parents regarding God's standard for Christian parenting. "Ye fathers" Gr: PATERES. It is the usual word for the male head of the family. Yet it does not exclude the mother. Like brethren is used by all Christians. Probably used "fathers" because the responsibility for managing a home and raising children is primarily theirs.

Paul divides this parental exhortation into two parts: negative and positive. Negatively, he says, "Parents, provoke not your children to wrath." Positively, he says, "but bring them up in the nurture and the admonition of the Lord" (v. 4).

There are two spiritual principles to Christian parenting:

A. Demonstrate the Quality of Gentleness! (v. 4a)

1. "And" is a definite shift from child to parent responsibility. If children are to "obey" their parents, parents must give them proper directions to obey. If they are to "honor" their parents, they must be worthy of that honor.
2. "Provoke" means "to irritate, to make very mad or angry." Sometimes refers to a lashing, open rebellion; sometimes to an internal smoldering resentment.
3. Parallel text: Col. 3:21.
4. Then the opposite to "provoke" is "encourage"; cautioned against being too severe with their children. In Bible days, parental authority was too austere, severe. Today, it is generally too lax, loose, and soft: A spiritual balance is what this Scripture calls for.
5. "Provoke" Gr: "vex, fret, overcorrect to resentment." "Provoke . . . to anger" suggests a repeated, ongoing pattern of treatment that gradually builds up a deep-seated anger and resentment that boils over in outward hostility.
6. Not usually intended, but thought to be for the child's good.
7. Here is the warning: "Don't provoke to wrath":

   a) By enforcing ridiculous, insignificant rules that tend to irritate.
   b) By neglecting to show your love for your children.
   c) By dealing too harshly or cruelly with them.
   d) By continually reminding your children of your sacrifices for them.
   e) By nagging and quarreling with them constantly. This is the home's greatest tragedy.

8. Remember! Things do change; the customs of one generation are not the same in another! Too much control is an insult to our upbringing of our children. Obligation is to give our children encouragement.
9. Show gentle firmness in discipline, but never exasperating, tantalizing severity. The parent who corrects when angry or in a rage provokes their children to hatred, rebellion.

B. **Demonstrate the Standard of Godliness! (v. 4b)**

Here Paul shows the spiritual responsibility of the parents in three words:

1. The Word "BRING THEM UP"!

   a) Another way of saying, "Raise, and nourish them to maturity."

   b) The first thing, realize their responsibility for their children. They are not our property! They do not ultimately belong to us! They were given to us by God for a while and for a purpose.

   c) For what purpose?

      1) Not that we may get what we want out of them. Use them simply to please ourselves.

      2) Not to gratify our own desires. Our business is to see that our children are raised, brought up, nurtured, prepared.

      3) Not only for a meaningful life.

      4) But also to a right relationship to God.

   d) "Bring them up" also suggests togetherness, a godly example. It is not a sending out but a going with.

   e) ILL: A little girl was walking home with her parents, holding her father's hand on a dark, eerie night. She suddenly asked, "Daddy, take my hand! I can only hold a piece of yours, but you can hold all of mine." In his strong grasp she seemed satisfied until she stopped again and asked, "Daddy, are you afraid?" He assured her he was not in the least. Then she started walking on cheerfully, "All right, if you isn't, I isn't." Oh, the greatness of life! A tremendous opportunity!

2. The Word "NURTURE"!

   a) "Nurture" Gr: "discipline." It is the idea of learning through discipline. It also means, "training, learning, instruction."

   b) The same Gr. word in Heb. 12:6 (PHILLIPS) is translated "chastening." Nurture is WHAT YOU DO to the children.

c) These are the rules and regulations which lead to the reward or the punishment. The child is rewarded for keeping the rule, and punished for breaking it.

d) To nurture is to train by rules and regulations, enforced by rewards and punishments.

e) It is necessary to train a child through discipline. If left to themselves, they will become rebels.

f) ILL: A few years ago a British statesman said, "Everything in the American home is controlled by switches, except the child."

g) Discipline in the right manner. In love, never in anger. May injure the body or spirit of the child. If we are not disciplined, we cannot discipline.

   1) ILL: Flying off the handle does for us what it does for a tool; it renders us useless.

   2) ILL: A teen once said, "My parents would use a cannon to kill a mosquito. I either get away with murder or get blamed for everything."

   3) ILL: A wayward girl once said, "I never knew how far I could go, because my parents never cared enough to discipline me. I figured that if it wasn't important to them, why should it be important to me?"

3. The Word "ADMONITION"!

a) Admonition is WHAT YOU SAY to your children. Gr: NOUTHESIA, "verbal instruction with a view to correct." ILL: "If you keep doing that, you are going to run into problems." "I must counsel you about that."

b) We are to teach our children with our words as well as actions. Nurture puts emphasis on actions. Admonitions on speech.

c) Talk to your children. Words of exhortation, warning, encouragement, counsel, advice, comfort.

CONCL: Most important phrase, "of the Lord." This puts Christian parents in an entirely different category than other parents. Not just good manners, commendable behavior, or general morality. The first thing in the parents' mind is that the children be brought to the knowledge of Christ as Savior and Lord. "Of the Lord" two meanings: "coming from the Lord" and "directed to the Lord."

ILL: A little girl came to her mother with the age-old question, "Mother, what is God like?" Mother hesitated and said, "You'd better ask Daddy." She asked, "Daddy, what is God like?" He too hesitated and evaded the question somewhat. Later on, in her childhood diary was found the entry,

"I asked my mother what God was like. She did not know. I asked my father, who knows more than anyone else in the world, what God was like, and he did not know. I think if I had lived as long as my mother and father, I would know something about God."

Parents do not have all the answers. But we must be able to show elementary Bible truths to our children.

Teach your children the Bible.

Insist on regular attendance to the house of God.

Practice your religion at home.

Lift your children to God in prayer.

Win them to Christ as soon as possible.

ILL: When the Supreme Court ruled against prayer in public schools, a Washington Post cartoonist published a cartoon of an angry father waving a newspaper at his family and shouting, "What do they expect us to do—listen to the kids pray at home?"

Absolutely, that is the place for Christian training. God wants to make our families all that they can be. He wants to keep us from getting pressed into the mold of the world.

Christian families should never fall apart. Christian marriages should always stay together. Our children should be happy. Our homes Christ-centered. A truly Christian home is the envy of the world. Children make their own choices which way they will go.

ILL: The first example of child-raising in the Bible should teach us that. We know that Adam and Eve were a sinful man and woman after the Fall. A sinful nature like we have. But they were undoubtedly model parents nonetheless. They were highly intelligent and knew God intimately. Moreover, they are numbered in the godly line of the age before the Flood, the line which contained such outstanding spiritual giants as Enoch, Methuselah, and Noah. There is no question but that they raised their children to know and honor God. Yet in spite of this, their first child, Cain, turned out to be a murderer.

Why? It was his choice to allow his old sinful nature to dominate his life.

ADDITIONAL NOTES: Faithful Parents

Be lavish and generous with praise for worthy accomplishments. Give compliments. Show them your approval.

ILL: A very successful painter, Benjamin West, tells an interesting story. When he was young, one day his mother went out, leaving him in charge of his younger sister, Sally. While mother was gone, he discovered some bottles of colored ink and decided to paint his sister's portrait. He made an awful mess—ink on everything in the room. But when his mother returned, she said nothing about the terrible ink stains all over everything. Instead, she picked up the piece of paper on which he had been working and exclaimed, "Why, it's Sally!" Then she stooped and kissed him. West often said, "My mother's kiss made me a painter."

Communication is essential to family life.

ILL: An 18-year-old girl told her pastor that her parents had not spoken to each other for years. Their only communication was note writing, the notes being delivered by the children. If they were in a situation where they had to say something to each other, the dad said it to a child, who repeated it to the mother. The mother gave her reply in the same way, through the child. This had been going on for years. Can you imagine the unhappiness of children in that home? The pastor asked the girl the obvious question. "When did this get started?" She replied, "It all started years ago when Mom and Dad couldn't agree on having the neighbors over for dinner."

Good advice for solving family problems.

ILL: The Apostle Paul gives some advice which all family members would be wise to remember. He suggests that all difficulties be settled on the same day they arise—before nightfall (4:26).

ILL: Four-year-old Andrew Roberts said to his father, Kevin, when he was about to spank him for disobedience, "Dad, you know this is going to cut into our relationship!"

IV. HARMONY AT WORK

Ephesians 6:5–9

INTRO: Some would rather forget these verses. They deal with secular work. Not important, personal, and private. However, this is God's inspired Word. It deserves and demands our complete attention and obedience.

This section began with the imperative (5:18), "Be filled with the Spirit." We get our stimulus from a different source—different from other men.

The Spirit-filled life is one of harmony. Harmony in marriage—husband-wife relationship. Harmony in the family—parent-child relationship. Harmony in the employee-employer relationship.

This passage is addressed to "servants and masters" with specific application to slaves and masters in the Roman Empire. Slavery was a part of the social and economic fabric of the ancient world. It is estimated that in the Roman Empire at this time there were 60 million slaves. More than half the population was enslaved to the other half.

It does not address the moral issue of slavery—its legitimacy or illegitimacy. Paul's chief concern here is the nature of the Christian's work. The Christian work ethic.

While the rightness or wrongness of slavery is not specifically discussed, some questions are raised:

1. Although Paul did not condemn slavery here, he did not condone it either.

2. The obedience to these transforming truths would inevitably lead to slavery's abolition.

3. The transforming view that all persons are made in God's image ultimately destroyed slavery.

It continues to transform work relationships even today.

Paul makes some strong statements regarding the nature of a Christian's employment, whether he is the employee or the employer.

A. The Duty of Christian Employees! (vv. 5–8)

What does a Christian employee owe his employer? These verses list a number of items.

1. The Christian Employee Owes His Employer OBEDIENCE! (v. 5a)

   a) Our first obligation is to please the Lord, and be a faithful testimony for Him. The Apostle says one way to do this is to give willing obedience to those under whom you work.

   b) Regardless of who they are or what their character is like.

   c) Being a Christian should always make a person a better, more productive, more agreeable worker.

   d) A Christian who does shoddy, careless work or is constantly complaining does damage to his testimony as a Christian.

   e) If an employment situation is intolerable, a Christian should quit and look for something else. But as long as he is employed, he should do the work to the best of his ability.

   f) A disobedient employee sins two ways:

      1) He is breaking his word to his employer

      2) He is robbing the company of unearned wages.

   g) "Obedient . . . in all things." All things not contrary to the company's rightful authority. All things not contrary to the Law of God and the gospel. All things not contrary to the dictates of conscience.

2. The Christian Employee Owes His Employer RESPECT! (v. 5b)

   a) Having the right attitude toward employment. The idea here is not a cowering fright but honor and respect that makes a person anxious to please. If not for the employer's sake, then for the Lord's sake.

   b) Often our place of work is a field of service for the Lord.

     c) Doing your work carefully and respectfully is a witness to the unbeliever, an encouragement to the believer, and a service to God.

3. The Christian Employee Owes His Employer SINCERITY! (v. 5c)

     a) Lat. SINE CERE "without wax." Actually proof of good quality.

     b) The word carries the idea of generosity and liberality, as well as sincerity. It suggests we should not hold back from our best but should pour ourselves out liberally in honest service.

     c) ILL: A personnel executive was interviewing a graduate, "I understand you are looking for work?" Graduate replied, "Oh, no, sir, I'm not looking for work, just a job."

     d) Too many people stop looking for work when they get a job.

4. The Christian Employee Owes His Employer LOYALTY! (v. 6)

     a) That's not easy to put into English: LIT: "Not only to win their favor when their eyes are on you, but like servants of Christ doing God's will from the heart."

     b) Here is a contrast: A person who works hard when the boss is looking and loafs along when he is absent; versus a steady, faithful service that comes from having the heart in the right place.

     c) ILL: An employer: "Look here, what did you mean telling me you had five years' experience when you've never even had a job before?" Young man, "Well, sir, you advertised for a man with imagination."

5. The Christian Employee Owes His Employer GOODWILL! (v. 7)

     a) Goodwill says it adequately. A Christian should work as if their "heart and soul" are in it.

     b) Does someone else have to do your work?

     c) ILL: Little Eldon, fretting at the teacher's assignment, asked skeptically, "Do you get paid for teaching us?" The teacher smiled, "Yes." The puzzled boy exclaimed, "That's funny! We do all the work!"

d) ILL: To succeed in your work, there are twelve things to remember:

1) The value of time
2) The success of perseverance
3) The pleasure of working
4) The dignity of simplicity
5) The worth of character
6) The power of pardon
7) The influence of example
8) The obligation of duty
9) The wisdom of economy
10) The virtue of patience
11) The improvement of talent
12) The joy of originating

B. **The Duty of Christian Employers! (v. 9)**

Christian faith does not create harmony by erasing cultural and social distinctions. There must be employees and employers; leaders and followers. Christian faith brings harmony by working in the heart. What does a Christian employer owe his employees?

1. He Must Seek Their Welfare!

a) Obedience to those over him, respect, sincerity, loyalty, and goodwill. Reciprocal duties!
b) He owes them fairness. It is the principle, "treat others as you want to be treated."
c) ILL: It is unfortunate when an employee has to say, "My boss is supposed to be a Christian, but you'd never know it."

2. He Must Not Threaten Them! "Forbearing treating . . ."

a) There are better ways to get cooperation than with threats of punishment.

b) He resorts to authority and power as little as possible.

c) He does not throw his weight around. Does not lord it over those under him. He is never abusive and inconsiderate.

d) He realizes his own authority/power is God-given, only functional and temporary.

e) He is accountable to the Master of all!

f) Heaven plays no favorites. No respect of persons with God.

g) All men are the same before Him.

CONCL: Christians must get it straight as to who they are working for and what their work is to be.

Some think it does not matter what I work at. But it does. There is employment for you that is challenging, fulfilling, where God can use you to His glory and to mankind's good.

What is your business?

ILL: William Carey was a shoemaker who applied to go as a foreign missionary. Someone asked him, "What is your business?" meaning to belittle him because he was not an ordained minister. Carey answered, "My business is serving the Lord, and I make shoes to pay expenses."

We are "servants of Christ, doing the will of God." He is then rewarded (see v. 8). Being a Christian is first priority!

ILL: A young man, who later was to become a world-renowned painter, was leaving home to get an education and pursue his career. His godly mother realized the spiritual pitfalls for such a young man in such a wicked world. Her last words to him as he left home were, "Son, remember, you were a Christian before you were a painter."

ADDITIONAL NOTES: Harmony at Work!

In our day, the struggle between employers and employees has reached monumental levels.

Conflicts rage constantly between workers and management, with each side accusing the other of selfishness and unreasonableness. Employees want smaller workloads, fewer hours, more vacation, and more pay and benefits. Employers want more productivity, more profits, and greater control of management policies and practices. Both sides want lower taxes for themselves while expecting greater government protection and subsidies.

It is not hard to see the heart of the problem on both sides is greed. The sin of greed is the primary fuel that feeds the inflationary spiral that has become a common part of modern life in most parts of the world.

When everyone wants more, prices must rise to pay for higher wages and profits. And as prices rise and money therefore buys less, people want still higher pay or profits to make up the difference.

When government becomes heavily involved in various subsidies and supports, then taxes, the national debt, or both must be raised. If the government prints more money without backing, the value of all its money is decreased, and again people want more income to make up the difference.

Added to all of that is the principle that as possessions increase, so does greed, because greed is by nature insatiable. It is likely that modern Western society is the greediest in history. Everyone wants more for less, and the ascending spirals of inflation and taxation are unabated.

How are such seemingly irreconcilable problems to be resolved? Many Americans are advocating some form of socialism, in which the gods have total control of the economy. As greed increases and self-interest becomes more hardened, more gods' control may be required to prevent anarchy.

Rev. 18 suggests that the final Antichrist will come into power through a great worldwide economic system in which virtually all power is centered in the hands of a few elite leaders.

But God did not design man's freedom to work against mankind. He designed it to allow us to earn a living, provide for our families, and be of service to others.

Man's depraved nature turns God's provisions to selfish ends.

V. WALKING IN VICTORY

Ephesians 6:10–13

INTRO: This section begins with "Finally, my brethren" (v. 10). With the use of the word "finally," Paul reaches the high point of this epistle.

In chs. 1–3 he had expounded the great doctrine of the church. How that God through Christ is gathering together all mankind in one body, the church.

In chs. 4–6 he has exhorted the practical life of the church. The worthy Christian walk. Walking in unity—purity! Followers of God. Walking in love—light—wisdom! Filled with the Spirit. Walking in harmony. In life's relationships. Harmony in marriage, family, and career.

Ends with walking in victory. Triumphant victory over Satan and all the forces of evil!

Now he says, "Finally, my brethren"! Don't misunderstand "finally." It is not used merely to end the letter. It is not a postscript, an afterthought. It has direct and immediate connection with the whole epistle.

Having expounded the doctrine of the church. Having explained the life of the church. After all that, the Apostle now says, "Finally, my brethren!"

Here is the doctrine—believe it!

Here is the life—live it!

Yet there is another important matter to consider. Another factor not yet named.

Here is the warning—heed it!

WARNING: You will face mighty opposition in this world of time if you believe the truth and live the life.

It is a stirring call to battle! Here Paul sets the silver trumpet of the gospel to his sanctified lips and sounds out a loud, clarion call to spiritual warfare.

The call can be heard in two strong notes:

A. The Inspired Instructions of the Spirit! (vv. 10–11a)

The idea here is preparation for battle. Get ready for a fight-struggle-conflict-warfare. The trumpet is clear on this point. (See 1 Cor. 14:8.)

1. The Clarion Call To Battle!

    a) Inward Battle (See Rom. 7:23.)
    b) Spiritual Weapons (See 2 Cor. 10:4.)
    c) Young Soldiers Enlisted (See 1 Tim. 1:18.)
    d) Fight Of Faith (See 1 Tim. 6:12.)
    e) Demands Consecration (See 2 Tim. 2:4.)
    f) Great Fight (See Heb. 10:32.)
    g) Called to: a cross, not a cushion; a pilgrimage, not a picnic; a fight, not a frolic; an execution, not an excursion.
    h) Each Christian is engaged in a great spiritual battle and must equip himself for it.
    i) Two contemporary problems:

        1) Some think salvation is not an entrance into warfare, but an escape from trouble of any kind.
        2) Others project the idea that the battle is all over and done with at Calvary by Christ. A proper balance must be struck. That balance is contained in . . .

2. The Companion Commands To Believers! (v. 10)

    a) Be Strong. There is no room for weaklings in Christ. (See 2 Tim. 2:1; 1 Cor. 16:13.)
    b) In The Lord! Not in yourself, in your belief, in your church. But in the Lord.
    c) In The Power Of His Might! It is His mighty power. Not human strength. (See Eph. 3:16; Mic. 3:8; Acts 1:8, 11a; Rom. 3:12; 2 Cor. 6:7.)

d) It is the whole armor of God. Not just part.

e) We are reminded by this combination of commands that we are unequal to the battle without the power of God and armor of God.

f) We have no strength. Our strength comes from the Lord. But equipped with His power and His armor, we can win every conflict in life.

B. The Invisible Enemy of the Church! (vv. 11b–13)

1. Now he tells us why we need the power and armor of God! (See vv. 11b–12.)

2. This does not at all deny that at times our struggle is at the human level. That is obvious. He is saying our conflict is not just on that level alone. We do have a visible human physical struggle. But there is a greater battle.

3. Here we are dealing with the ultimate cause of the world situation: The disease, not just the symptoms.

4. The problem is not merely on the human level. The human battle is but the symptoms; the real cause is farther back. There is an invisible warfare going on against the devil and his evil forces.

5. Paul repeats the word "against" five times for emphasis! Not grammatically correct. Modern editors would delete the repetition and maybe a whole lot more. It is God's way of emphasizing that in this spiritual warfare the Christian is "up against it."

6. There are invisible foes, and we must fight against them.

a) We Must Fight Against "The Devil!" (See v. 11b; 1 Pet. 5:8.)

1) He is called "the accuser of our brethren" (Rev. 12:10). Chief activity.

2) Adversary: He is against us, an opponent, a foe, the leader of an army set against us. "Prince of the power of the air" (2:2).

3) He is "the tempter." As such misleads, deludes, seduces us.

b) We Must Fight Against "Principalities-Rulers!"

1) This reveals the devil's control of certain regions. A ruler governs a certain territory. Like human rulers over different countries.

2) Demons must operate this way because they are not omnipresent as God is.

c) We Must Fight Against "Powers—Authorities!"

1) Authority and rule are not the same.

2) One may have great authority, yet not rule.

3) Authority has to do with values. It says the values of our culture, as well as specific territory, are demonically controlled.

4) Seems to be repeating "principalities-rulers."

5) Assigned by Satan to rule specific territory in the world. The rulers of the darkness of this world.

d) We Must Fight Against "The Rulers Of The Darkness of This World!"

e) We Must Fight Against "Spiritual Wickedness In High Places!"

1) TR: "the spiritual forces of evil in the heavenly realms."

2) The emphasis here is upon the evil of this spiritual control. The forces we struggle with are wicked and destructive.

CONCL: Such a secular and materialistic world denies these spiritual forces. But indeed forces stronger than himself stand behind what is visible. Such as poverty, hunger, war, oppression, sin, and immorality.

Why is man so wicked? Why is all this? Why do people behave this way? What is wrong with the nations always at war, building up armaments capable of destroying the whole world? What is the cause of such widespread immorality? Why the collapse of values we are seeing all around us?

There is only one answer! It is the unseen rulers of darkness who are manipulating world affairs.

It is not just unjust men. It is the unseen spirits of evil. We are not wrestling against men. We are wrestling against the unseen powers that are behind it all.

Satan and his cohorts! The demons of hell! The forces of evil!

Victory is ours! "Resist the devil, and he will flee from you" (Jas. 4:7).

See 1 Pet. 5:8–9; Rev. 12:9, 11.

You must stand after every victory! "Having done all, to stand."

Be sober. Be vigilant. Respect your enemy. Do not relax. Do not go on vacation. There is no vacation in spiritual warfare.

Stand. Pray. Be steadfast. But when you must take your stand, you are offered the armor, the power to "stand," to "withstand" and "having done all, to stand."

Our Captain commands: Be Strong! Put on the armor! Take your Stand!

ILL: Orders are not for discussion! The British General Montgomery believed in obedience. When he came into command in North Africa to rescue his forces from dreadful defeat, he expected his commands to be carried out to the tee. He said, "Orders no longer form the basis for discussion." Previously, orders had generally been questioned by subordinates right down the line. He determined to stop this state of affairs at once. The general discovered the cause of the lost battles in Africa.

ILL: More Than Conquerors! When Lord Nelson reported to the British government his great victory over the French fleet in the Battle of the Nile, he said "victory" was not a large enough word to describe what had taken place.

When Paul spoke of the victory we have through Christ over the struggles, conflicts, adversaries, temptations, and woes of life, that greatest of all words, "conqueror," was not sufficient to describe it; therefore he said, "more than conquerors through him that loved us" (Rom. 8:37).

VI. OUR REAL ENEMY

Ephesians 6:11–12

INTRO: We need the truth about the devil. No lies here!

ILL: Two boys were walking home from SS. The lesson had been on the devil. One asked, "What do you think of this devil business?" Other answered, "Well, you know how Santa Claus turned out, don't you? It's either your mother or your dad." We need the truth about the devil, our real enemy!

The Intelligence Corps plays a vital part in warfare because it enables the officers to know and understand the enemy. Unless we know who the enemy is, where he is, and what he can do, we have a difficult time defeating him.

It is reported that many psychiatrists and psychologists now believe in the existence of a personal devil, who just a few years ago strongly denied it. They give three reasons for the change:

1. The sheer reality of evil present in the world.

2. The actual witnessing of exorcisms from people possessed by a super-human evil spirit.

3. The existence of people who love evil, and practice evil for its own sake.

Those who know the Bible are not strangers to any of these facts which verify the existence of Satan and his evil forces. Whether it's the OT at the dawn of time, the gospels, or the book of Revelation, the Bible emphatically affirms Satan's existence and his activities.

This is Paul's purpose in these verses, to show the real enemy that stands behind the enemies we see in our daily spiritual struggle:

"Put on the whole armour of God, that ye may be able to stand against the wiles of the devil. For we wrestle not against flesh and blood, but against principalities, against powers, against the rulers of the darkness of this world, against spiritual wickedness in high places" (vv. 11–12).

This passage reveals three important truths about OUR REAL ENEMY, the devil:

A. Satan is a Great and Powerful Foe!

1. This is seen in the words used to describe his agents: "principalities—powers—rulers of darkness—spiritual wickedness or evil forces." Also, we are warned to take up arms "against" them.

2. When we talk of the devil being "great and powerful," we must not overstate the case. Because he is a spiritual being rather than physical like man, we tend to think of Satan as more or less God's equal. It is true he is a counterpart to the greatest of the unfallen angels: Michael or Gabriel. But he is not a spiritual counterpart to God.

3. God is God alone. Every other being is created by God. And therefore limited for the simple reason that they are created.

   a) God Is Omnipotent—All-Powerful.

      1) The devil is not. God can do anything.
      2) The devil can only do what he is permitted to do.
      3) This is God's universe, not the devil's.
      4) Even hell is not the devil's; God created it for the devil and his angels.

   b) God Is Omnipresent—All-Present! (See Ps. 139:7–10.)

      1) This cannot be said of Satan.
      2) The devil can only be in one place at one time. He must work through demons, the other spirit beings who fell with him.
      3) Though the devil's influence is widespread, probably none of us here have ever been tempted by the devil directly.

4) The Bible records only 6 persons who were so tempted: Eve (not Adam), Job, Jesus Christ, Judas, Peter, and Ananias (not Sapphira). There indeed may have been others, but these are the only ones specified in the Bible.

c) God Is Omniscient—All-Knowing!

1) He knows everything.

2) This is not true of Satan. Satan does not know everything. Undoubtedly, he knows a great deal. And he must be a shrewd guesser. Yet the ways of God must constantly surprise him. He knows no more about what is going to happen in the future than we do.

3) Yet Satan is powerful. He is called "the ruler of demons"; "the prince of this world"; "the prince of the power of the air"; "the god of this world." A great dragon, a roaring lion, the vile one, the tempter, the accuser, the Lie, the spirit working in the children of disobedience.

4) Satan and his forces are an evil, formidable, cunning, powerful, and invisible foe against whom no human being in his own power is a match. But he can be resisted and overcome by the blood of Christ and the Word of God.

5) ILL: Think of Adam and Eve before the Fall. Perfection. Excelling us in intelligence. Spiritual consciousness. Close to God. Yet they fell.

B. Satan is a Wicked and Destructive Seducer!

1. He is the "prince of the power of the air" (2:2) that stands behind "the darkness of this world" and the "forces of evil [spiritual wickedness] in the heavenly realm" (v. 12 NIV).

2. Satan's Manner Is Evil And Wicked!

a) The devil is behind every evil deed and thing in this world. He is the king of darkness.

b) He is in command of the forces of evil. He traffics in everything that would defile the human race: alcohol, drugs, war.

3. Satan's Goal Is Destruction! (See John 10:10.)

    a) Satan's mission: steal, kill, and destroy persons, homes, families, lives, communities, and countries.
    b) His final goal is to destroy every soul in hell.
    c) Remember, Satan and his demons have no moral principles, no code of honor, no higher feelings. They are utterly unscrupulous and ruthless in the pursuit of their malicious designs.

C. Satan is a Sly and Crafty Deceiver!

1. His activity towards believers is called "the wiles of the devil" (v. 11). Unfortunate TR: "wiles" Gr: "schemes, devices." Gr: METHODIA, from where we get our English method.
2. The idea is of craftiness, cunning, deception. (See 4:14.)
3. ILL: The term was often used of a wild animal who cunningly stalked and then unexpectedly pounced on its prey. Satan's schemes are built around stealth/deception.
4. It speaks of his elaborate plan of evil against believers. (See 2 Cor. 2:11.)
5. Satan Is Crafty When He Attacks! Someone suggested there are six times in life when Satan is more likely to attack:

    a) When the Christian is newly converted.

        1) Early days of Christian life are glorious, alive with desire, freedom, optimism, joy.
        2) That's when Satan comes. When one is not yet confirmed in the paths of obedience. Trips them up.
        3) Then he says, "You have sinned, you are not a Christian; conversion was temporary, you have fallen, no hope now; settle back in and follow me."

    b) When the Christian is afflicted.

        1) When things go wrong is the right time for Satan.
        2) He accuses: "If God loved you, you wouldn't suffer like this. So give in."

c) When the Christian has achieved some notable success.

   1) Self-confidence after some victory.
   2) Tempted to self-reliance.

d) When the Christian is idle.

   1) If the devil finds a man inactive, he will soon find some work for him to do.
   2) Idle hands are the devil's hands.

e) When the Christian is isolated from other believers.

   1) In the company of the saints there is safety, strength, fellowship.
   2) Separately, Satan will break us.

f) When the Christian is dying.

   1) It's the last-ditch effort. Satan's last chance.
   2) He will come to the dying at their weakest moment to defy them.

6. Satan Is Crafty In How He Attacks!

   a) Satan comes as a roaring lion. (See 1 Pet. 5:8.)

      1) Here Satan appears before us with a frightful roar, to terrify us into forgetting who we are and whom we serve.
      2) ILL: A liberal preacher, denying Satan's existence, said, "I am not afraid of the devil." A Christian replied, "But is Satan afraid of you?"

   b) Satan comes as a friend. (See Gen. 3:5.)

      1) He did not come threatening, but with an offer to help out.
      2) Show them what God is like. Make them "like God, knowing good and evil" (Gen. 3:5 NIV).

   c) Satan comes as an angel of light. (See 2 Cor. 13–15.)

1) Satan comes bringing "enlightenment." You don't believe those old-fashioned things, do you? Many pulpits are guilty.
2) ILL: Martin Luther, "When you look for the devil, don't forget to look in the pulpit."

CONCL: Satan is indeed a terrible enemy. Yet we have no reason to be downcast, discouraged, or despairing. God has given us the victory, if we arm ourselves and stand true to the end.

ILL: Here is the secret. Do not trust in yourself. The Apostle Peter did, and he fell. In his own self-strength he said, "Even if all fall away, I will not" (Mark 14:29 NIV). But that very night, Peter, who considered himself the strongest of all the apostles, denied his Lord three times, on the last occasion even with oaths and cursing.

ILL: The purpose of Lucifer's (Satan's) rebellion was to become omnipotent. His recorded five-fold intent in Isa. 14:13–14 shows that purpose:

1. "I will ascend into heaven."
2. "I will exalt my throne above the stars of God."
3. "I will sit upon the mount of the congregation."
4. "I will ascend above the heights of the clouds."
5. "I will be like the most High."

He had mentioned heaven, the stars of God, His holy mount, the clouds of His glory. But yet he goes farther and declares his intention towards God Himself. Lucifer would be like God.

One of the highest of God's creation, the wisest and most beautiful, aspired to be higher still.

He was wise, but he wanted to be omniscient, to know all.

He was powerful, but he wanted to be omnipotent, to be all-powerful. He was capable of going anywhere in God's universe, but he wanted to be omnipresent, to be everywhere. In short, Satan wanted no authority, no presence, and no glory above his own.

His original intent was to obtain omnipotence.

If he could attain that goal, he would be unequaled in the universe, for it is impossible to divide omnipotence.

If two things are equally powerful, neither can be said to be all-powerful. Two equal powers cancel each other. Omnipotence must stand alone. Only God is omnipotent. God is God alone.

VII. WINNING THE VICTORY

Ephesians 6:14–20

INTRO: Paul has warned us of the warfare, described the enemy, and now shows us how to win the victory.

You can win the victory in every spiritual battle!

Human nature would opt for the easy life, and sign a truce with the world, the devil, and the flesh. That will never work for a real Christian.

The Christian life is warfare. Battle. Struggle. Conflict.

We have a real enemy! The devil. Adversary. Prince of demons. Prince of this world. Accuser. Deceiver. Seducer.

There are the forces of evil. The demons of hell. Principalities. Powers. Rulers of darkness. Spiritual wickedness in high places.

Satan and his forces are a formidable foe! His intent is to destroy souls. We must fight against him. To do so, we must be properly armed and equipped to win the victory and defeat the enemy.

ILL: Paul writes this epistle from prison. Here he suddenly sees a ready-made picture. Chained to the wrist of a Roman soldier. Night and day the soldier is there as his guard. The soldier's armor suggests a picture to him. Paul takes the armor of the Roman soldier and translates it into Christian terms.

- The Belt of Truth defends us vs. any and all error!

- The Breastplate of Righteousness defends us vs. false accusations of hypocrisy!

- The Sandals of Peace guard us vs. cowardliness in witnessing (taking a stand) for Christ!

- The Shield of Faith protects us vs. the fiery darts of the wicked.

- The Helmet of Salvation protects us vs. intellectual error and rationalistic doubts of salvation.

These are the five parts of our defensive armor vs. satanic attack. This arsenal is available for our defense.

Four times Paul repeats the word "STAND" (vv. 11–14). In these five items of armor, this passage gives us the principles of our defense in time of spiritual struggle.

If we are to STAND against the wiles of the devil in the wicked day, the fiery days of the wicked, there are five essentials:

A. We Must Know for Certain the Absolute Truth! (v. 14a)

1. The Belt of Truth defends us against any and all error that may attack us. We are protected by the Knowledge of Truth!

   a) "Truth" Gr: ALETHEIA basically refers to the content of that which is true. The content of God's truth. This knowledge is essential in our battle vs. the schemes of the devil.

   b) The word can also refer to an attitude of truthfulness, integrity, and genuineness. However, knowing the truth produces truthfulness, integrity, and genuineness.

2. We are "girded in truth," established in that element, wrapping it around us. The "belt" secured all other items of armor and allowed freedom of movement.

3. Decision: "Let God be true, but every man a liar" (Rom. 3:3). Jesus to Thomas: "I am the truth." (See John 14:6.) Jesus Christ is the Truth. Truth about God, man, life, death, sin. Not a truth, but the truth.

4. Satan violently attacks the fundamentals of truth. Inspiration of the Bible is denied. Deity of Christ questioned. Atoning blood rejected. Resurrection discredited. 2nd Coming heresy. Heaven a myth. Hell nonexistent.

B. We Must Make a Firm Commitment to Right Living! (v. 14b)

1. The Breastplate of Righteousness defends us against the evil accusations of hypocrisy. Protected by righteous living.
2. The "breastplate" was a tough sleeveless piece of armor that covered the soldier's upper body. It was often made of leather and covered with metal. It gave protection to the heart and other vital organs.
3. It is not self-righteousness, "filthy rags" (Isa. 6:4). It is Christ's righteousness. The righteousness of God by faith. It also includes practical righteousness of a life lived in obedience to God's Word.
4. Right living is a great defense against Satan's attacks.
5. Words are not defense vs. evil, but a good life will stop the mouths of the gainsayers.
6. ILL: A good Christian was once accused of certain crimes. "What will we do?" He answered, "Well then, we must live in such a way as to prove the accusations are a lie."
7. The believer is impregnable when clothed in righteousness.

C. We Must Always be Ready to Stand Up for the Gospel! (v. 15)

1. The Sandals of Peace guard us against cowardliness in taking our stand for Christ. Protected by a firm stand.
2. "Preparation" Gr: HETUIMASIA has the general meaning of readiness.
3. A good pair of boots allows the soldier to be ready to march, climb, fight, or do whatever else is necessary.
4. The Roman Military Sandal was clotted with nails that gripped the ground firmly, even when it was sloping or slippery.
5. The sandal is the preparedness of (caused by) the gospel of peace. The good news of peace keeps us steadied, upright, and firmly grounded.
6. ILL: Preparation suggests promptness and readiness. We are God's minutemen. Grounded in the gospel of peace. Ready to obey orders at a minute's notice. Equipped and ready to move.
7. Eager to share the gospel with those who have not heard. Ready to share the experience of salvation with those who are not saved.

8. Prepared to share Christ with those who may not know Him.

D. We Must Hold Fast to a Simple Trust in God! (v. 16)

1. The Shield of Faith or trust in God protects us vs. the fiery darts of the wicked. Protected by trust in God.

    a) The shields in Roman warfare were twofold: large, oblong body shield; small, round chest shield.
    b) The large, oblong body shield was made of wood covered with leather. The "fiery darts" were flaming, poisonous darts used in battle. They were caught by the wooden shield and put out upon entering the leather.
    c) Just as the Roman soldier held and trusted his shield of wood, we must lay hold of the promises and put our trust in God.

2. "Faith" here refers to a basic trust in God for daily provision and help. To Paul, faith is always a complete trust in Christ.
3. ILL: When John Paton was translating the Bible for a South Sea Island tribe, he discovered they had no word for faith. One day a native who had been running hard came into the missionary's house, threw himself upon a large chair, and said, "It's good to rest my whole weight on this chair." Paton said, "That's it, I'll translate faith as resting one's whole weight on God."

E. We Must Know for Sure (We are Saved)! (v. 17)

1. The Helmet of Salvation protects us against intellectual error and rationalistic doubts. Protected by the assurance of salvation.
2. The fact that the "helmet" is related to "salvation" indicates how Satan's blows are directed at the believers' assurance of salvation. Satan swings his "broadsword" at the believer's head. It has two dangerous edges: discouragement and doubt. The assurance of salvation will keep us from mental, intellectual, and rational errors, doubts, and discouragements.
3. Salvation is the head-covering. (See Ps. 140:7; 1 Thess. 5:8; Eph. 2:5, 8.)

4. Salvation is a "renewing of the mind." (See Rom. 12:2.) The war rages in the battle for the mind. That is the decisive battle in this war. As a man thinketh, so is he. (See Prov. 23:7.) Confused minds are vulnerable to Satan's attack.

CONCL: Note the phrase "the whole armour of God." It is both divine and complete. We cannot win in our own strength. God has provided completely for our victory.

The armor is already provided (vv. 11, 13)! It says "TAKE" not MAKE the armor. It is divinely provided and ready to be "put on." All we need to do is "take up" and "put on" this equipment.

The Christian soldier is armed from head to foot with defensive armor. There are a belt, a breastplate, shoes, a shield, a helmet. They stand for truth, righteousness, readiness, trust, and salvation! This is all we need for victory in any spiritual battle.

But it is worthy to note there is no armor for the back. There is nothing for the back. He that turns his back to the enemy to run is defenseless. Doomed to fall.

Retreat and turning back are not alternatives in spiritual warfare.

See Luke 9:62 and Heb. 10:38.

Remember to "STAND" in time of battle:

Know the truth!

Commit to right living!

Share your faith!

Trust in God!

Know you are saved!

That is God's provision. Divine and complete. Take it. Put it on. Victory is yours!

VIII. WEAPONS OF OUR WARFARE

Ephesians 6:17–20

INTRO: Victory is not isolation from the world. It is insulation against the evil. Jesus prayed, "I pray not that thou shouldest take them out of the world, but that thou shouldest keep them from the evil" (John 17:15).

Our defense against evil is "the whole armour of God"; "the armour of light" (Rom. 13:12). (See also 2 Cor. 6:2.)

If we are going to win the victory, stand against the schemes of the devil, withstand in the evil day, hold out against the fiery darts of the wicked, we must know the truth; commit to right living; stand up for Christ; trust in God; and be sure about salvation.

1. The Belt (truth) arms us against Satan, The Liar! Equipping us with a bold, certain knowledge of truth. Knowledge of what is true. Truthfulness. Integrity. Genuine.

2. The Breastplate (righteousness) vs. Satan, The Accuser! Living such a good life as to silence any accusation of the wicked.

3. The Sandals (peace) protect us against Satan, The Serpent! Equipping us with preparedness, readiness, eagerness to stand up for Christ, share the gospel.

4. The Shield (faith) arms us against Satan, The Tempter! Equipping us with a simple trust in God in every circumstance of life.

5. The Helmet (salvation) arms us against Satan, The Deceiver! Equipping us with an assurance of salvation that none can doubt. There can be no confusion here.

Now this passage presents us with the offensive weapons of our warfare. We use them in attack against the forces of evil. The pieces of armor are all defensive. The weapons are offensive. We can have a holy boldness! (See 2 Cor. 10:3–4; Heb. 4:12; 1 Sam. 17:45.)

These alone are offensive: "the sword of the Spirit, which is the Word of God" (v. 17); and the mighty weapon of prayer.

A. The Word is Our Mighty Weapon! (v. 17b)

It is "the sword of the Spirit" because the Spirit gives it, inspires it, and uses it. The Word of God can pierce the inner man just as a material sword pierces the body. The hearers at Pentecost were cut to the heart. (See Acts 2:37; 5:33.)

1. Meaning of Word—What It Is!

    a) "Word of God" Gr: not LOGOS referring complete, all of the word. That is the LOGOS, the Word of God that stands behind everything we see, and governs it.
    b) John used this word when he spoke of Jesus Christ (see John 1:1–14).
    c) The Gr. here is RHEMA, referring, not to all the Word, but to the particular Word for the specific situation.
    d) ILL: Have you ever had the Spirit give you a Word (RHEMA) from the Word (LOGOS) that exactly fit the circumstances of your life? That is the sword of the Spirit given to soldiers in combat for use against the enemy.

2. Meeting of Satan—How To Use It!

    a) Paul's idea is modeled by the victory of Jesus over Satan in the wilderness of temptation.
    b) ILL: The devil approached Jesus at the end of a 40-day fast when He was hungry. (See Matt. 4:3.) It was not wrong for Jesus to use supernatural power to produce food. In fact, His first miracle was changing water into wine; two times He multiplied loaves. The problem was it would have been wrong for Him to use His power to test the word of God. The "if" is the problem. Just before this at His baptism, God had said, "This is my Son" (see Matt. 3:17). Immediately, Satan comes with, "If thou be the Son of God." The temptation was to doubt the veracity of God's Word.
    c) Jesus quoted Deut. 8:3 in Matt. 4:4.

d) Satan says good point! And in the second temptation he quotes Scripture. (See Ps. 91:11–21 in Matt. 4:5–6.)

e) Do you believe? I believe it so much, let's go to the highest point of the Temple. What a rip-roaring start for your ministry! "Jesus said unto him, It is written again, Thou shalt not tempt the Lord thy God." (See Deut. 6:16 in Matt. 4:7.)

f) Jesus used Scripture to interpret Scripture. An important principle in Bible study. In effect, "Satan, you want me to put God to the test. But you must understand it is not God who is to be tested. I am the one being tested. My responsibility is not to test, but to trust, God."

g) On the third try, Satan threw all subtlety to the wind and revealed his real goal. After he had shown Him the kingdoms of the world and their glory, he asked (Matt. 4:9), "All these things will I give thee, if thou wilt fall down and worship me." In final triumph, Jesus said (Matt. 4:10), "Get thee hence, Satan: for it is written, Thou shalt worship the Lord thy God, and him only shalt thou serve" (see Deut. 6:13).

h) In all the Bible there is not a better example of the power of the specific sayings (RHEMA) of the Word of God to defeat Satan. If God's own Son had to know the Word of God, how much more we must know the specific sayings of Scripture, have them memorized, to overcome.

B. The Weapon of Prayer is Our Secret Resource! (v. 18)

The weapon of prayer—praying in the Spirit. It is not turning over a grocery list to God. Effective prayer is always in the Spirit. Prayer is contact with HQ! A soldier must not lose contact with his captain. Prayer is the energy that enables the Christian soldier to wear the armor and wield the sword.

1. Prayer is the power for victory. But not just any kind of prayer. Here is how to pray if we are to defeat Satan.

2. Notice the three "ALLS" in the use of the weapon of prayer:

   a) "ALWAYS!" On all occasions. Consistent. Constant.

1) Begin by asking, "When do you usually pray?" Most everyone, Christian or not, will pray in difficulty.

2) Far too often the prayer life of Christians is no better than that. A hurried, goodnight prayer. Thanks before plunging into a meal. But they really pray when things go bad.

3) ILL: They are like the man who was asked what position he assumed when he prayed. He answered by explaining how he had once fallen into a well headfirst and had gotten stuck head down in the mud at the bottom. He said, "The pray-ingest prayer I ever prayed, I prayed standing on my head." Pray in the good times and in the bad times.

b) "ALL PRAYER!" All kinds of prayer. Intense. Fervent.

1) Different kinds of prayer: supplication, intercession, thanksgiving. If we ask for things only, we are missing out on the blessings that come from intercession and thanksgiving.

2) Praise is a great weapon for defeating Satan. "Praise changes things." Intercession for others can bring victory to our own lives. (See Job 42:10.)

3) ILL: A good formula for prayer. Acrostic of the word ACTS. ACTS stands for A-doration, C-onfession, T-hanksgiving, and S-upplication.

c) "ALL SAINTS!" Unselfish. Generous.

1) How many saints is that? There is no list available. All the saints in the body of Christ around the world. All the saints who are suffering, those in positions of power with their special temptations, isolated saints, saints of different ethnic and cultural backgrounds.

2) ILL: The Lord's Prayer begins with "our Father," not "my Father."

3) We are actually praying for other members of the family of God.

4) Now Paul adds a specific request. (See v. 19.) And he adds an interesting addendum. (See v. 20.) Pray for your preacher. Not for his comfort, but power.

5) We pray too much for ourselves, and not enough for others. Learn to pray for others and with others.

CONCL: Complete spiritual victory is ours in all of life's circumstances if we: Know the Word and use it; Know how to pray and do it! These are the weapons of our warfare!

Notice effectiveness in both depends on the ministry and power of the Holy Spirit. It is the Holy Spirit who gives us a particular part of the Word of God just when we need it. It is praying in the Spirit that is effective! What does it mean, "praying in the Spirit"? The answer is given in Rom. 8:26–27.

A great Christian said, "Groanings which cannot be uttered are often prayers which cannot be refused."